PLANET ZOO

*one hundred animals
we can't afford to lose*

PLANET
ZOO

*one hundred animals
we can't afford to lose*

Simon Barnes

illustrated by Alan Marks

Orion
Children's Books

This is for Joe, in the hope that all 100 species
will bring him joy

SB

First published in Great Britain in 2000 by Orion Children's Books
a division of the Orion Publishing Group Ltd
Orion House
5 Upper Saint Martin's Lane
London WC2H 9EA

Designed by Sarah Hodder

Printed in Italy by Printer Trento S.r.l.

I owe a lot of people a lot of thanks for help with this book. First thanks to Alice, Leila and Leyla for reading and making helpful and supportive comments on the manuscript. I owe a mighty lot of thanks to Lucy Farmer of the Worldwide Fund for Nature, for her support, contacts and time. Jo Mee, librarian at the World Wildlife Fund (WWF), was also a tremendous help. I have had an enormous amount of help from many people in conservation organisations: there are so many people in the world who want to share their knowledge, and forward the cause, and it is a privilege to know and work with these people. These include Peter Jackson of the Cat Specialist Group at the International Union of Nature Conservation, Sian Pullen from WWF, Chris Harbard, Mike Everett and Martin Davies from the Royal Society for the Protection of Birds, Kathleen Rosewarne of Birdlife International, Simon Forrester from the Wildlife Trusts, Chris Breen of Wildlife Worldwide, and Baron Robert Stjernstedt of Tongabezi. Finally, thanks to CLW, without, as ever, whom, etc. etc.

Contents

Contents

1 Scimitar-horned oryx

DINOSAURS were my favourite animals, of course. Weird, amazing, wonderful, ugly, beautiful, enormous, tiny – and dead. Extinct. Gone for good. No living human has ever seen a dinosaur: and no human ever will.

We can't bring back dinosaurs. Extinction is for ever.

What happened to wipe them out? People now believe that a huge meteor, whirling through space, crashed into the planet Earth, and laid waste to the place. It was worse than the worst atom bomb ever made. Goodbye dinosaurs: goodbye practically everything. The big things vanished for ever, but some of the small insignificant things survived. Life on Earth today sprang from the small and insignificant things that survived the great extinction.

It wasn't the first time it had happened. It was only the most recent. There have been five major extinctions in life's history. Five times, the Earth has been hit by a mega-disaster, by a massive Extinction Event when vast numbers of animal species were lost for ever.

The sixth great extinction is happening right now. All around us. Every day. The first five great extinctions were violent acts of nature.

Nobody can do anything to stop a meteor in its tracks. But today's Extinction Event is the act of human beings. And we can stop it right now. Can? We must. For the animals' sakes, for the world's sake, for our own sakes.

Which brings me to the time I saw a unicorn. Yes, I *know*, they are imaginary beasts. They never existed: they are just a weird and lovely poetic idea. But I have always been haunted by unicorns. I once saw a cartoon, in which Noah sailed away in his Ark on the rising waters of the flood – leaving behind him a pair of unicorns, animals that, it seems, had somehow failed to go two-by-two into the ark. A very sad cartoon. As if the lovely unicorn had gone extinct, not through wickedness, but through sheer carelessness.

That is roughly what is happening in the world right now. Our own sheer carelessness could do for us all.

But back to my unicorn. It looked like a horse. It moved like a horse. It trotted, it cantered, and I saw quite clearly the long, slender horn rising from its head. I knew it couldn't be a unicorn, of course. All the same, it was moment of pure magic. The animal turned a little and I could see then that it had the usual number of horns, two of them, and it was an antelope: an oryx, master of the desert.

The people of the Middle Ages made collections of animal stories. Many of the stories were untrue (if poetical); many of the animals were unreal (if beautiful and weird). Such a collection was called a bestiary. This is my bestiary; but all of the stories are true (*and* poetical) and all of the animals are real (*and* beautiful *and* weird).

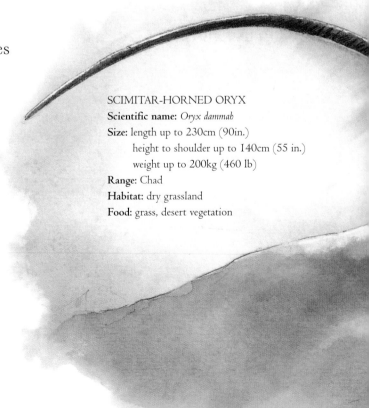

SCIMITAR-HORNED ORYX
Scientific name: *Oryx dammah*
Size: length up to 230cm (90in.)
        height to shoulder up to 140cm (55 in.)
        weight up to 200kg (460 lb)
Range: Chad
Habitat: dry grassland
Food: grass, desert vegetation

Most of us go through a dinosaur period. Well, the animals I shall bring you in this book are certainly weird, amazing, wonderful, ugly, beautiful, enormous, tiny – and *nearly* dead. On the very edge of extinction. Let's not moan about it, though. Moaning helps nobody and nothing. Let's enjoy every bit of their weirdness, beauty, ugliness and so on – and then let's get on with the job of saving them. They are not dinosaurs, no – and they are not going to go extinct, either. Not if we can help it.

If I can't start with a unicorn, I shall start with the next best thing: well, even better, since it is real and it still exists. Just. This is the **scimitar-horned oryx**, and it was once very common. It lives in the Sahara desert, and the legend of the unicorn almost certainly came from this lovely antelope. In 1936, someone saw a herd of 10,000 scimitar-horned oryx. Ten thousand unicorns!

Since then, most of them have been shot. Hunting has done for them: hunting for food, more than for what some people call fun.

The big herds have split and scattered, so the animals now hang on only in odd pockets and forgotten corners. They need safe reserves. If reserves can't be set up, the scimitar-horned oryx will become an animal that dies of human forgetfulness – just like the unicorn in my never-to-be-forgotten cartoon.

People used to fear the wild animals and the wild places of the world. Now, almost too late, we have learned to look after them. Once, humans fought desperately against nature. Now we fight desperately on nature's side. We see now that it is our job to look after the wild places: just as it is a keeper's job to look after the animals in a zoo. Wild animals are not there for our amusement: but they are certainly our responsibilty. We are all now keepers in Planet Zoo.

2 Kakapo

THIS book contains 100 species of animals. There are plenty more species in the world than that, of course, and plenty more in danger of extinction. I am just scratching the surface. How *many* species of animal are there in the world? I must confess, I always thought that if you went to the right sort of library, or accessed the right kind of database, you would be able to find a list. All the species of animal in the world. A nice fat volume: all animal life on Earth within its covers.

The list does not exist. It never could exist. The best we can come up with is a rough guess. There are about 4,000 mammals, including us humans. More than 9,000 birds; 30,000 other chordates (amphibians, reptiles, fish); 80,000 molluscs; 6,000 echinoderms; 73,400 arachnids. There are 750,000 species of insects alone, and 290,000 of them are beetles. And these are only the animals that are 'known to science'. It's an exciting phrase, is it not: 'previously unknown to science'? I always thought that scientists opened a bottle of champagne when they discovered an animal that was 'previously unknown to science'. But they don't - because they're discovering them all the time.

In fact, it has been calculated that there are approximately 1.4 million living animal species that are, indeed, 'known to science'. And science has been at it for a long time, so there can't be many more left, can there? Wrong. Most scientists agree that there are *at least ten times that number of animals.* Science itself has only scratched the surface.

We're trying to save the Earth, and we hardly know what's in it. The Earth is a huge subject: and its theme is change, difference, variety, diversity: endless forms most beautiful. The buzzword for all

KAKAPO
Scientific name: *Strigops habroptilus*
Size: length up to 64 cm (25 in.)
      weight up to 3.5 kg (7.75 lb)
Range: New Zealand
Habitat: dense scrub-forest, grassland
Food: many different kinds of plants
      and flowers

these things is *biodiversity*: the endlessly different ways in which life on Earth happens.

There are two themes to this book: one is biodiversity. The other is Not Giving Up. The two come together in the sad, happy, and altogether ridiculous story of the **kakapo**.

The kakapo is the bird they gave up on. In the early 1970s, they decided that the poor thing was extinct. Then, in 1976 they discovered that they were wrong.

The kakapo is, if you can imagine such an absurd thing, a flightless parrot. The idea of a flightless bird seems silly enough, I know - why bother to be a bird, and not fly? But many birds have developed flightlessness. Their ancestors fly, or are blown by the wind, to remote islands. There, they find a safe world. Flying takes a huge amount of energy: defying gravity is hard work. It is more expensive, after all, to run an aeroplane than a car. So the birds take the easy option, and stop flying.

That's what happened to the ancestors of the kakapo, when they came to New Zealand. And they grew big and heavy, and developed a weird mating system. The male makes a small bowl in the earth and makes a booming sound, and waits for the female to turn up.

And often, she does not. This odd system actually worked in their favour for years: it made sure there were never too many of them for their islands to get overcrowded with kakapos. And they were safe, as they crept about on the forest ground in their clownish fashion, because there was nothing to eat them.

Until humans came along, bringing with them, by accident and on purpose, cats, rats and stoats. And they also brought animals that competed with the kakapos for food and space: possums, deer, chamois. The kakapo had found a very successful way of living a quiet life; but suddenly, and through no fault of its own, everything changed. The goalposts of evolution had been shifted.

Most of the surviving kakapos have now been taken by humans to smaller islands, where the danger of the introduced animals is much less: Codfish Island, Barrier Island. People who care - the word for them is conservationists - have set up programmes for managing these islands in a way that gives the kakapos the best possible chance. For a start, they keep out cats, rats and stoats. The world has done its best for the kakapo. But the fear is that it might just have done it too late.

3 Tiger

THERE cannot be a person in the world who is not thrilled by the idea of the **tiger**. And it is a fact of life that the more thrilling the animal, the more people want to save it, the more they are willing to give money, the more they will speak up for the cause of conservation.

Conservation means saving things, and few animals have more goodwill going for them than tigers. Most people have never heard of the scimitar-horned oryx and the kakapo, and so they can't get very excited about the idea of saving them. But who can resist a tiger?

Why, then, is it in danger? It is an animal that thrills the world: also, it certainly looks like an animal that knows how to take care of itself. How can an animal as fierce as the tiger find itself in danger?

The answer is in the question. Big fierce animals are always rare. They have to be rare. They could not exist if they were not rare. The chain of life starts with the sun, which gives the energy for the plants to grow. There are animals that eat the plants. And there are animals that eat the animals that eat the plants.

Life on Earth is a great deal more complicated than that, of course. But that is how the basic system of life operates.

Now, there are many more plants than there are animals to eat them. If the animals ate all the plants in their area – in their ecosystem – then they would have nothing left to eat, and the plants would not grow back again. And the entire ecosystem, and everything that lives in it, would die. This is actually happening in some places when people keep too many domestic animals, as we shall see later.

And just as there are more plants than plant-eaters in a working ecosystem, so there are very many more plant-eating animals than animal-eating animals. In an English wood, there are more leaves than caterpillars, more caterpillars than caterpillar-eating blue tits, and perhaps just one sparrowhawk that eats blue tits.

The big fierce animals are always the rarest. They are, in fact, *always* on the edge of extinction. The more fierce you are, the more vulnerable you are. And tigers are as fierce as they come.

Everywhere you find it, the tiger is the animal on top: the number one predator. And this is a way of life that is filled with difficulties. When something goes wrong, the little animals tend to suffer, but there are still many that survive. It is the biggest and the fiercest that find the going toughest. If the number of deer in a forest in India is halved, you still have half the deer. But with only half the deer left, the tiger may starve to death.

The tiger is the world's biggest cat; but it lives in Asia, the continent with the world's fastest-growing human population. People need land for their farms, for their houses, for their industries. They

may not think too highly of sharing their land with a beast that kills people. The tiger is under constant pressure from humans.

And the fact that the tiger is so thrilling brings another danger. Chinese medicine – and we shall meet this problem again and again – is made from many natural ingredients, such as plants, fungi, bits of dead animal. And it so happens that Chinese medicine believes that wine made from tiger bone is a wonderful tonic. People will pay a lot of money for tiger bone wine, and that means that a dead tiger is worth a fortune. Tigers are protected practically everywhere they exist: but people still shoot them, and take away their bodies to make medicine.

There are conservation programmes for the tiger all over Asia, including Siberia, where you find the biggest race of tigers in the world. There are police and game wardens whose job is to stop people shooting tigers. But the appetite for tiger bone wine continues, and so does the illegal shooting. It will continue until the makers of Chinese medicine can be convinced that the world will run out of tigers if they carry on selling tiger bone wine – and can be convinced that it matters. That is a job conservationists are now beginning to take on.

TIGER
Scientific name: *Panthera tigris*
Size: head and body length up to 2.8 m (9.2 ft)
tail length up to 94 cm (37 in.)
weight up to 300 kg (660 lb)
Range: Asia, east of Afghanistan
Habitat: wide range of habitats; anywhere
so long as it can find water, cover and prey
Food: animals up to twice its own size

4 No-eyed big-eyed wolf spider

NO DOUBT you think I have made this one up. But I promise you – there really is an animal called the **no-eyed big-eyed wolf spider**. I don't need to make it up: the truth is much weirder than anything I can invent. But that doesn't mean that the world of animals is weirder than you imagined. The fact is, it is weirder than you *can* imagine.

Now let us clear something up before we start. This species of spider comes from a large group of spiders that hunt down insects, overwhelm them and eat them. That's why they are called wolf spiders. There is a family of wolf spiders that tends to have big eyes, so they are called the big-eyed wolf spiders. But this is a freakish member of this family that lives in the perpetual darkness of a cave in Hawaii, and it is blind. And so you can see that, in a slightly crazy way, the name no-eyed big-eyed wolf spider makes sense.

Many people do not care for spiders. These people have my sympathy. I am not frightened of spiders – so I keep telling myself, anyway – but I don't really warm to them. I always remember the time when I spent a night in a hut in Africa, and counted on the ceiling no fewer than 45 spiders. And yes, they were wolf spiders: many of them as big as a spread hand. I didn't look to see whether or not they had big eyes.

Many people would be happy if they never saw a spider again. But does that mean we might as well kill off the spiders? Many people dislike bees and wasps. What would happen if we killed all of them as well? First, no one would ever get stung again. And second, most of the flowering plants would die. They need bees to spread their pollen.

Plants depend on various fliers and buzzers and creepies and crawlies. They could not survive without them. Humans need plants to feed themselves and to feed the animals they keep for food. Humans could not survive without plants; that means that humans could not survive without insects.

But could humans survive without the no-eyed big-eyed wolf spider? Well, as a matter of fact, we probably could, without much trouble. These spiders – refreshingly small spiders – live only in the deepest part of the Koloa cave in Hawaii. They need a very damp atmosphere to survive. But people are taking the deep water from below the ground and using it to water their crops, mostly sugar cane, which means the caves are drying up.

Would it matter if the no-eyed big-eyed wolf spider went extinct? It would to them, obviously. And it would matter to the scientists who study the bizarre life-systems that operate in the pitch black of these extraordinary caves. But they don't really benefit humanity a great deal, do they, these little blind spiders? So why should we bother with them?

It's a huge question. But if we look at it another way, it is no question at all. Why should we need to prove that any species is useful to human beings? Quite apart from anything else, the web of life, the massive biodiversity of the planet, is bewilderingly complex, and everything in it is interlinked in a wildly complicated and chaotic fashion – which means that it is quite impossible for anyone to prove that any given species is *not* 'useful'.

Every species is important, and every ecosystem depends on everything in it. What's more, every ecosystem on the planet depends on every other ecosystem. The planet operates, not as a series of sealed rooms, but as a vast open house, in which all who live there depend on everything and everybody else. Earth is not a series of parts but a colossal whole.

The no-eyed big-eyed wolf spider is a tiny bit of the whole, living in a tiny corner of a particularly tiny room. Important? No. Essential? Certainly.

NO-EYED BIG-EYED WOLF SPIDER
Scientific name: *Adelocosa anops*
Size: body length up to 20 mm (0.78 in.)
Range: Hawaii
Habitat: caves
Food: insects and other invertebrates

5 Orang-utan

ET'S go from one of the tiniest and least crowded rooms in the house of the Earth, to the most crowded room of all, the rainforest.

Rainforests – that is to say, the hot, moist forest found mostly at the equator – occupy six per cent of the land surface, which is not so much, not when you compare it with the oceans, which cover 75 per cent of the entire planet. But the point about rainforests is that they contain more than half of the species of organisms that make up life on Earth. Every rule of life we discuss in this book, every single principle of conservation: all these count double when you come to rainforest.

Everywhere on Earth seems like a desert after you have been to a rainforest. The richest habitat in the world is a poor apology for life, after rainforest. Rainforests are so full of life, it's frightening.

And talking of being frightened, I shall never forget the pair of eyes that stared me down from a small hiding place in a tract of rainforest on the island of Borneo. Human eyes, they seemed to me, though golden; dark leathery face, and he looked as if he had just swallowed a dinner-plate. That was a male: the face-plate a signal of his maturity and strength. It meant, don't mess with me. I didn't.

I was looking at an **orang-utan**. A large ape, related to chimpanzees, humans and gorillas. Did the golden eyes see me as a fellow-ape? Perhaps so, but orang-utans have little cause to love the human species.

ORANG-UTAN

Scientific name: *Pongo pygmaeus*
Size: standing height up to 150 cm (59 in.)
    weight up to 100 kg (220 lb)
Range: Borneo, Sumatra
Habitat: tropical forest
Food: mainly fruit; also leaves, shoots, insects,
    bark, eggs, baby birds, baby squirrels

Orang-utans live in the rainforests of Borneo and Sumatra. They have been hunted, captured for zoos and circuses and as exotic pets. But the real problem is the loss of their homes. The rainforests are being destroyed, in Asia, and everywhere else.

If a wild animal is to survive, it needs a place to live. And not just anywhere. A kakapo needs the wet, cold New Zealand forests; a no-eyed big-eyed wolf spider needs its moist Hawaiian cave; an orang-utan needs the hot, moist, teeming rainforests of the tropics.

There are some good and effective conservation schemes in place for the orang-utan. There are a number of reserves in which the animals are protected, and with them, the places where they live. And one of the joys of this is that if you save an area of forest for the orang-utans, you save it for everything else as well: for the trees, for the strange frogs that live in the canopy, for the birds that live high up in the tops of the trees and never see the ground or think about going down there, and for the countless thousands of species of creepy-crawlies, the endless numbers of them that are still unknown to science.

But the rainforests continue to be cut down. The timber is very valuable; but the trouble with a rainforest, even more than with most habitats, is that once you have destroyed it, it is gone for good. It won't just grow back. A rainforest is the result of 50 million years of growth. In that unimaginably long period, tree has succeeded tree, on and on through the centuries. To put it back together would take millions more years, and it could not possibly be the same, even if left unmolested. And the orang-utans don't have the time to wait.

Orang-utans need rainforests: so, for that matter, do humans. Rainforests are the biggest mass of green growing matter on the planet. The destruction needs to be stopped, for all our sakes. Why?

Well, there are more kinds of plants in the rainforest than there are in any other place on Earth, and – since most medicines originally came from plants – there might be a plant that cures cancer. But we have a much stronger argument than that. We are back to the notion that on Earth, everything depends on everything else. The great bulk of the surviving rainforests passes out colossal quantities of water, as an invisible mist, as water vapour. The rainforests provide the planet with a cool sunshade. If we cut down our rainforests, we start to fry. Rainforests are not only full of life in themselves: they help to make life possible everywhere else.

6 American bison

ONCE flew in a balloon over the Serengeti plains of Africa. I have never seen so many really big animals all together: wildebeest, the African antelopes that look like cows gone mad. About a million of them, if you are counting, and in the basket beside me an American sighed in the silence and said, 'This was the Midwest, once.'

He was talking about America. And he was talking about the **bison**, or buffalo; it is the same animal. When the West was wild, the plains and the forests of North America were filled with bison.

In the Serengeti there are times when the wildebeest fill up every scrap of land you can see: horizon to horizon, nothing but wildebeest. And the American was right: there was a time, not long ago, when bison did the same thing in North America.

For years people have believed that everything in North America was peaceful and beautiful until Europeans came in with their guns. This is not the way it was. In North America, over a period of two million years, 50 large species of mammal went extinct. But over the last 12,000 years, things speeded up dramatically. During this time another 57 species of large mammal followed them into extinction.

These are extraordinary figures. So what happened? What set off this catastrophic change? Humans happened. People once thought humans were unable to cause serious damage to other animals until they invented guns. But humans, with spears and poisoned arrows, with pits, and above all, with their ability to work together, were a devastating force long before they invented gunpowder. A favourite tactic was to surround a herd of animals, and to drive them over a cliff. You didn't have to be big and fierce, you didn't need a gun. You just needed to be smart.

The point I am making is that the great wave of extinctions is not a recent thing. It has been happening for years: it has been happening for longer than any normal history book can tell us. Now modern technology gives us many more ways of killing things. But now we also have the wisdom, the experience – and the technology – to stop the destruction in its tracks.

So far, the record of human beings is that the better the technology, the more rapid the pace of destruction. The bison, already hunted hard by the people who lived in America before the Europeans came, was more or less wiped out when the guns arrived.

AMERICAN BISON
Scientific name: *Bison bison*
Size: head and body length up to 3.8 m (12.5 ft)
　　　height to shoulder up to 2 m (6.5 ft)
　　　weight up to 1,000 kg (2,200 lb)
Range: Canada, USA
Habitat: plains, grassland, woodland
Food: grass, sedges, leaves

About 200 years ago, there were still more than 50 million bison. Demand for space, demand for meat, demand for fur: the animals were shot. Killing off bison was also a way of getting rid of the old way of life of the native American population.

The bison were caught in the crossfire. They died by the million. And there is no going back to the time when 50 million bison could roam at their ease. There is no place left for them, among the towns and cities and freeways and the farmland and the factories.

But the tide turned before it was too late. Just. There are small bison populations in various protected places. There are up to 2,000 in Yellowstone National Park; others in smaller reserves and private ranches. There are about 5,000 more bison in Canada. They can be bred in captivity, and, if given protection, can be released back into the wild, where they can survive and do well. This is not possible with many species of animal, but it suits the bison.

The American bison once roamed the continent, and humans lived in small isolated pockets. Now it is the other way round: a vast place for humans, with small pockets of wild places with wild animals. At least people now realise what these places are. They are treasures.

7 Megamouth shark

PERHAPS the best name in this book, after the no-eyed big-eyed wolf spider, is the **megamouth shark**. Maybe you have never heard of the megamouth shark. Well, until 1976, no one had heard of it. The beast is a pretty decent size, but no one had a clue that such a thing existed.

And the only reason that humans ever got to find out about this beast is the purest accident. It happened that a research vessel from the United States Navy was working in the Pacific Ocean near an island called Oahu. It was using a large parachute as its anchor, and something got tangled up in the parachute. They managed to lug the whole lot onto the boat, using the arrangement the boat normally used for pulling torpedoes out of the water. And there they found an absolutely colossal fish that no one had set eyes on before. It was over four metres long and weighed nearly 75 kilos.

It had a huge head, and a mouth to match, so the name they gave

it was a very good one. But the megamouth of the beast is not used for eating human bathers, or even for eating other fish. The sea is full of tiny specks of life, animal and plant, called plankton. The megamouth shark must feel as if it is swimming through a very weak fish soup – a kind of fishy vacuum cleaner, forever taking in these little specks of life.

We have been taught to think of sharks as if they were all undersea monsters, forever waiting to devour swimming humans. The great white shark is certainly ferocious enough, and many horror stories have been told about it. But there are about 350 different kinds of sharks, and they range from whoppers to tiddlers. The very biggest, the whale shark, weighs five tons, and never in its life does it eat anything that is bigger than your fingernail; it is a filter-feeder, like the megamouth. One of the tiniest, the cookie-cutter shark, is less than half a metre long – and much fiercer.

The discovery of the megamouth shark is a nice story. How many more megamouths are down there? Simple answer: not a clue. A few more have been discovered, completely by chance. Are there a lot down in the deep water, vacuuming away? Or are there very few, are we down to the last one or two? Are they thriving? Are they on the edge of extinction?

MEGAMOUTH SHARK
Scientific name: *Megachasma pelagios*
Size: no average size (not enough specimens found)
  Those caught have measured around 4.3 m
  (14 ft) and weighed 750 kg (1,650 lb)
Range: unknown, specimens have been caught in
  the western Pacific Ocean
Habitat: ocean
Food: shrimps, perhaps other forms of plankton

The oceans cover 75 per cent of the earth, as we have seen. We know little enough about the richness of life on land and we know a great deal less about life in the oceans for the obvious reason that it is much harder to get to the bottom of the ocean than anywhere on land. The deeper and darker the ocean, the less we know about what lives there. How many more undiscovered giants are swimming about down there? How many monsters have gone extinct in the depths, without humans even knowing they existed?

The oceans are filled with mysteries. The 350 species of shark continue the great theme of life on Earth: the word, once again, is biodiversity. And the chance discovery of the megamouth proves, once again, that biodiversity is greater than we ever thought.

8 Mallorcan midwife toad

THE age of extinction continues, and most of the animals under threat come from faraway places: the depths of the ocean, the islands that dot the vastest seas; the rainforest. Those of us who live in Europe or North America, or in the great cities of the world, don't have so many endangered and exotic animals living under our noses. This isn't because we have looked after our pieces of the world any better. Quite the contrary: we have already got rid of most of the animals.

We are not responsible for the actions of people who lived before us. We are responsible for what is alive now. This becomes a problem when rich and developed countries turn to poorer countries and say: you must look after your rainforest. And they get the reply: you got rid of your forests – the great wild woods of Europe, the wild places of the North American continent. And it made you rich. Why shouldn't we do the same?

It's a fair question. But the world is wiser than it was in the days when people destroyed the forests of Europe and America. And the remaining wild places belong to the world. We – that is to say, all the world – must take responsibility for saving the wild places: and responsibility means, so far as the richer countries are concerned, money. Money must come from rich countries and go to poor countries to make worldwide conservation possible.

It also means that we must look after our own endangered animals with especial care. Which brings us to the charming beast called the **Mallorcan midwife toad**.

MALLORCAN MIDWIFE TOAD
Scientific name: *Alytes muletensis*
Size: up to 5 cm
Range: Mallorca (Spain)
Habitat: mountain torrents
Food: tadpoles filter food from water;
adults eat insects and other invertebrates

The toads are European citizens, but they live in one of the few wild bits that Europe has left. They can be found only in the precipitous mountains in the north of the Spanish island of Mallorca. They have their peculiar name because of their peculiar habits. The toad father does the job of caring for the young – the young being, of course, the eggs. It's his job to give his eggy children the best possible start in life. And so he carries a ribbon of eggs around with him after the female has laid them. They stay with him, twined around his legs, for several weeks. When the time comes for them to hatch out, the father finds a suitable pool among the torrent streams of this mountainous place, and turns the eggs away. They are just ready to hatch, and so, by his efforts as midwife, he has saved the eggs from being eaten. The tadpoles are given a flying start to their lives by this ingenious arrangement.

This species is another one that was thought to be extinct; until 1980 they were known only from fossils. They live, however, on the very edge of extinction: a small population of just 500 pairs, restricted to a few mountain streams.

As the human population on Mallorca rose, so the toad population shrank. Humans naturally helped themselves to vital water and generally altered the toads' habitat. They somehow introduced a water-snake to the island, and the snakes eat toads. All bad news for the Mallorcan midwife toad.

What the toads need is a safe (and wet) place to live. Luckily they have a champion or two: their cause has been taken on by the Jersey Wildlife Preservation Trust, an organisation that has never restricted its interests to the cuddly animals, and also by Frankfurt Zoo. These organisations know the value of thinking small. They have been able to breed the toads in captivity, and have started a release programme, hoping to re-establish toad populations in the places where they have died out.

Conservation is a global problem: terrifyingly large. Look at it all at once, and it seems quite impossible – we may as well give up now. But we don't. We know that the best way to begin is by thinking small.

9 Numbat

IT is time to strike a blow for marsupials. Marsupials are perhaps the most misunderstood group of all the world's mammals. Marsupials are the pouched animals: kangaroos, wallabies, koalas. There are a few in South America, and very many more in Australia.

With most mammals, the young are born more or less fully formed: they do most of their early developing and growing inside the mother's body. Marsupial young are born as blobs, and they develop outside the mother's body, normally, as with kangaroos, in a pouch.

Since this is different from the way that humans produce their young, there was a time when humans tended to look down on them. *Lower* mammals, they sneered. A sort of mistake. And when a species of marsupial was edging towards extinction, there was a kind of shoulder-shrugging process that went on: well, what do you expect? Marsupials are doomed anyway: walking and hopping failures.

It all came from the notion of the ladder of progress and it's all complete nonsense. People used to believe – some still believe – that life is a ladder, with bacteria on the bottom, insects in the middle, and mammals on the top. And in this very top group, the marsupials are on the bottom. And guess which species we always place on the topmost rung of all? That's right: human beings.

But life is not really like that. Bacteria are the oldest life-forms around: they have survived for 3,500 million years, without bothering to change much, or develop or progress or to evolve more complicated bodies. We like to call the present day the Age of Mammals, just as there was once the Age of Dinosaurs. But in terms of numbers of species, numbers of individuals, and sheer persistence, the history of life on Earth has always been the Age of Bacteria; and always will be.

Marsupials are not failed mammals. In fact, kangaroos thrive so effectively that they are regarded in many areas as pests. And where marsupials are in trouble, it is not because their system of rearing their young in their pouches is unable to meet the vigorous challenges of modern life. It is because, once again, humans have moved the evolutionary goalposts.

And that is the case with the **numbat**. The numbat is an oddity within an oddity: a marsupial that does not have a proper pouch. The young, the little numbat blobs, simply cling to their mothers' fur, holding tight to her nipples.

Marsupials come in a great range of sizes, and a great range of different lifestyles. Kangaroos are enormous; the numbat is about the size of a big rat, and it lives entirely on termites. The mother carries her young everywhere she goes for six months, by which time they are too big for her to lift. So she leaves them in a safe place, generally a hollow log, and returns to tend them each night. She does this for another four or five months; almost a full year of intense mothering.

These days, numbats are found only in a small corner of a single Australian state. There are probably fewer than 2,000 of them left. They live in eucalyptus forest, and like plenty of hollow logs to hide in, and plenty of termites to eat. Captive numbats have been known to eat 20,000 termites a day. But many forests have been cleared for agriculture; and the forests

NUMBAT

Scientific name: *Myrmecobius fasciatus*
Size: length 23 cm (9 in.), plus tail 18 cm (7 in.)
 weight up to 600 g (21 oz)
Range: Australia
Habitat: eucalyptus woodland
Food: termites

that remain tend to be managed – that is to say, tidied up. A tidy forest has very few logs lying about, and therefore very few termites. The numbat has other problems as well: European immigrants introduced foxes and domestic cats to Australia. Both are happy to feed on numbats.

It is not that numbats are no good: the problem is that humans, by managing forests and introducing predators, have altered their world.

Altering it back is very difficult: but it is beginning to happen. The first thing to do is to protect the eucalyptus forests that remain, to manage them in a more natural fashion, and to make sure they are free of foxes and cats. Numbats respond well to captive breeding, and are being moved back to areas where they once lived. The numbat is not after all a small failure. It is a small conservation success story: or at least, the beginning of one.

10 Asian elephant

M OST of the human history that we read tells us about great human achievements. But there is another side to the story. Perhaps humans are not so cosmically important as all that.

Consider the sight of the stars on a clear night, when you are away from towns and roads and the glare of human lights: endless and uncountable millions, and within those millions, millions more. And the sun just a small star in the middle of it all; and the Earth just a small chunk of matter whirling around it, and humans just a small species, one that has been around for just a million or so years – nothing, compared to the hundred million years in which the dinosaurs were the dominant large animals on Earth. It takes a lot to make a human humble, but a really good look at the stars will do it for you. Another way of feeling humble is to consider the length of time dinosaurs dominated the Earth.

Yet another way is to meet an elephant. Its sheer size is enough to make the biggest human that ever lived feel small. An elephant is strange: it uses its nose as a hand and its ears as a cooling system. But there is something we have in common with elephants at the same time: we are both mammals, we both like to live in sociable groups, we care for our young. Elephants are believed to be the only non-human animals with an understanding of death; they have been observed burying their dead. Like us, they mainly seek only the peaceful life.

It is hardly surprising that the **Asian elephant** plays an important part in the religious life of Asia. Every year, in Sri Lanka, a domesticated elephant carries the eye-tooth of the Lord Buddha, a sacred relic, in a procession. One of India's best loved gods is Ganesh, the elephant-headed bringer of good fortune.

An elephant inspires awe, affection, even reverence. But that is not enough, because an elephant also needs space. The Asian elephant is smaller than the African, but it is still colossal and it still needs a colossal amount of food. The elephant's eating strategy is basically to pass as much food through its system in a day as possible. It has been estimated that an adult Asian elephant needs about 140 kilos of grass,

ASIAN ELEPHANT
Scientific name: *Elephas maximus*
Size: height to shoulder up to 3 m (10 ft)
weight up to 2,270 kg (5,000 lb) for females,
5,400 kg (11,900 lb) males
Range: Asia, from India eastward to China
Habitat: prefers forest with permanent water supply
and grass
Food: more than 100 species of plants

bamboo, bark, roots and leaves every day.

That requires a great many plants, and therefore a great deal of space. And as the human population of Asia continues to grow, space is the most valuable thing on the continent. Africa still has vast spaces; Asia does not. That is why – despite the fact that African elephants are poached for their ivory – it is the Asian animal that is in deeper trouble.

Forests are cleared for farmland. Elephants, deprived of their natural homes and food, raid the farms. Farmers demand that elephants are shot, to protect their businesses. There are now only between 34,000 and 54,000 wild Asian elephants left, and the deep forest areas they need continue to shrink.

So what is being done to help the Asian elephant? Awareness of the problem is a good first step. The way forward is to reduce tensions between people and elephants. There are now some good programmes for elephant conservation, at local and at international levels. It would be a bad idea to lose the few remaining animals that can make humans feel humble.

11 African wild dog

ADOG, we hear, is man's best friend. If that is the way he treats his friends, it must be a hard job to be his enemy. The English language is full of doggy expressions: and practically all of them are filled with unkindness and contempt. 'I wouldn't,' people say on hearing of some particularly terrible treatment given to a fellow human being, 'treat a *dog* like that.' A person in disgrace is said to be in the dog-house. To call a man a dog, or for that matter, to call a woman a bitch, is a terrible insult.

This is a poor reward for several thousand years of close association between our two species. Admittedly, some dogs have always been prized, as hunters, as family friends. And today, the richer parts of the world are filled with beloved family pets. But even here, tales of the cruelty and neglect handed out to less fortunate dogs are, for the animal charities, a matter of weary routine. Dogs have given humans a more or less uncritical friendship: and their reward is contempt. If we treat our domestic friends like this – how will we treat dogs that live in the wild?

The answer is: shoot them to the brink of extinction. It is what has happened to the **African wild dog**. The African wild dog is not, in fact, a very close relation of the domestic dog. Its motley coat is strange indeed, and its massive, radar-tracker ears give it an unfamiliar look. But all its movements are doggy; its expressions and its body language are doggy; and its air of friendliness and sociability among its companions in the pack reminds us inescapably of the animals that we bring into our homes.

African wild dogs once roamed in their packs over much of Africa. They have a complicated social life, one based on sharing and caring. Only one male and one female in the pack actually breed and produce young. It is the job of the rest of the pack to help feed and care for the pups. Hunting is a shared effort: a single dog alone cannot kill much in the way of prey, but a pack of wild dogs is capable of outrunning big animals and bringing them down. Back at the den, all the dogs in the pack will help to feed the pups.

It is a charming system in some ways; in human terms, an admirable one. And yet the dogs have been shot all across Africa. The reason for this is to be found in a single word. Vermin. The word is a terrifically emotional one. An animal that is accepted as 'vermin' can be treated any way you please. It is the animal equivalent of 'weed': a flower we can dispose of as we wish.

'Vermin' means that normal rules of care and respect do not apply. Wild dogs were seen as vermin, and killed without compunction.

Human contempt for dogs was doubled for these wild ones. They were not just inconvenient: they were dirty dogs, offensive to humankind. Those who shot wild dogs felt that they were doing the world a favour.

There are other reasons for the decline of the African wild dog. Dogs are roamers, capable of covering huge distances; stamina is part of their lifestyle. A pack of wild dogs in the Serengeti uses a territory of 1,500 square kilometres. As human populations spread, and farming increased, so there was less room for wild dogs, and more people to shoot them. Wild dogs are also prone to all the diseases brought to them by domestic dogs. This means that even in protected areas like the Serengeti, wild dogs are pretty rare.

Luckily there has been a change of attitude since those carefree days of mass shooting. As African open spaces begin to be lost, so the big national parks have been protected from the developers. Africa has the luxury of developing later than some other countries. Africa can, if it chooses, learn from the mistakes of history, the mistakes which Europe and North America made centuries ago.

African wild dogs need space as the first priority in their conservation; and Africa still has some space. It is in the vast remaining spaces of Africa that these dogs, and many of the other great animals of the world, still have hope. Still have a future. They must be cherished, these places. And we must watch them like hawks. We talk about saving animals: time and time again, we come down to the nitty-gritty, saving not animals but places. If we can only save the wild places, we will be saving many, many species of wild animal.

AFRICAN WILD DOG

Scientific name: *Lycaon pictus*

Size: height to shoulder up to 79 cm (31 in.)
head and body length up to 112 cm (44 in.)
tail length 41 cm (16 in.)
weight up to 36 kg (79 lb)

Range: Africa, south of Sahara

Habitat: bushland, open and wooded savannah

Food: antelopes, zebras, warthogs, occasionally
rodents and small mammals

12 Spectacled bear

'YOU destroyed your forests, so why shouldn't we clear ours?' Let us return to the rainforests and to this nightmare argument. As we do so, we consider a very clever, smart and adaptable bear. It is called the spectacled bear for the good reason that it looks as if it is wearing a pair of giant glasses.

It is true, as we have seen, that the developed world, Europe and North America, destroyed most of its ancient forests. They can never be put back. Welcome to the Humpty Dumpty Effect.

An ecosystem, once destroyed, cannot be put back together again. People have tried; always, they have failed. Scientists call this the Humpty Dumpty Effect; naming it for Humpty's great fall. 'All the king's horses and all the king's men, couldn't put Humpty together again.'

An ecosystem is more complicated, more diverse, than humans can imagine. A forest is more, a great deal more than a few trees, especially a rainforest.

We know this now. But nobody knew this when the great forests of the north were chopped down. We know now about the important part played by forests in keeping the Earth cool. But nobody knew then. Nobody could imagine that any place anywhere in the world could ever possibly run out of trees.

But now we know. And still we clear rainforests. The humans of early ages could not possibly know that the forests they destroyed would be gone for ever. But those who clear forests today know. And they continue the destruction, pretending that the truth does not exist. There is a difference, a very great difference between ignorance and wilful blindness.

The spectacled bear is victim of wilful blindness. A little bit more forest destruction won't hurt. Everyone else is doing it, so why shouldn't I? If I don't, somebody else will. So the forests are cleared and the richer countries permit them to be cleared, because they do not believe it matters enough to make a fuss. In this way, every day the planet becomes a little poorer.

The spectacled bear likes rainforest best, forest at around 2,000 metres. But unlike most rainforest animals, it is very adaptable. It can live in all sorts of different places as well. It can cope with near-desert, and also with mountains, places where you never see a tree.

It lives in South America: Bolivia, Colombia, Ecuador, Peru; and there are a few left in Venezuela. The main problem is habitat destruction: no home, no bears. The bears also suffer from direct persecution: hunted for meat and for sport. They have also been shot, because they are considered vermin. In fact, the bears eat mainly fruit and plants; also insects and small rodents. But the bear, being an adaptable beast, may occasionally take domestic animals like chickens, in places where humans have moved into bear country.

The bear needs space. The spaces exist, but they are being destroyed. Proper protection is needed for the places where the bears live. If the rich countries do not join with the poor countries – that is to say, if the countries that have money do not join forces with the countries that have forest – then the forests will go. We, they will continue to tell us, destroyed ours.

Someone did, but it wasn't us. It was people who died long ago, people who knew nothing of what we know today about the natural world and the way the planet works. It is too late for these forests. The Humpty Dumpty Effect has taken its toll. But the destruction of the tropical forests can be stopped. It is not too late yet.

Only nearly.

SPECTACLED BEAR
Scientific name: *Tremarctos ornatus*
Size: body length up to 1.8 m (6 ft)
shoulder height up to 86 cm (34 in.)
weight up to 160 kg (350 lb)
Range: Panama and South America
Habitat: very adaptable and can live in many
different habitats, from rain forest to
near desert
Food: fruit, plants, insects, small rodents

13 Bumble-bee bat

THERE are many ways to fly. Humans have invented machines that fly in quite different ways: jets, propeller-driven aeroplanes, helicopters, microlights, powered gliders. The animal world has even more. Birds and insects have found many different ways of beating gravity.

And so have mammals. Flight is so amazing that it opens a new world of possibilities. And that is why bats are one of the most successful groups of mammals around. If you judge success by the number of different species thrown up by a group – its biodiversity – then bats are the most successful mammals after the rodents.

If you can fly, you can get anywhere in the world, and bats have done exactly that. It is sometimes said that before humans arrived, there were no mammals at all in New Zealand. This is wrong; there were bats. But bats are often overlooked, mainly because of their dark, rather mysterious lives. They are at home in the dark: humans are not.

Bats fly without the use of feathers: they do not so much fly as swim through the air. It is not the near-perfect method that is used by the birds. Nature isn't a story of perfection. Certainly, many aspects of animal-design *look* like perfection; a humming-bird wing, or a vulture's, being good examples.

But nature is about finding solutions to problems. Nature's creatures do not have to be perfect: they just have to work. And the bat's wing works. It is, in short, Good Enough: good enough in fact to allow the bats to form hundreds of different species. There are bats as big as ravens, and they live in flocks that darken the sky when they move out together. There are tube-nosed bats, whose nostrils form long tubes. There are disc-wing bats that have suckers on their thumbs,

BUMBLE-BEE BAT
Scientific name: *Craseonycteris thonglongyai*
Size: head and body length up to 33 mm (1.3 in.)
wing span up to 17 cm (6.7 in.)
weight up to 3 g (1 oz)
Range: Thailand
Habitat: caves near bamboo thickets and
teak plantations
Food: small insects

so that they can perch head-down on a sheet of glass, should they so wish. There are many bats that eat insects, many more that eat fruit. But there are a good few oddballs as well, as you would expect in a group with so many species. There are fish-eaters, and bird-eaters. There are the hare-lipped bats that eat other bats. And of course, there are the famous vampire bats of tropical America, that can only digest blood.

The tiniest bat of all is probably the most endangered. This is the **bumble-bee bat** from Thailand, sometimes called Kitti's hog-nosed bat. It is one of the smallest mammals in the world, with the body of a fully-grown adult not much more than 3 centimetres long. The wings, however, are more than 15-17 centimetres across, with long tips that allow the bat to hover. By night, bumblee bats hunt tiny insects. By day, colonies of about a dozen individuals roost in small caves in western Thailand.

Bat-spotting is difficult work. The bumble-bee bat was not even discovered until 1974, by which time it was already in deep trouble. The forests of Thailand where the bats originally lived have mostly been destroyed for agriculture. It is likely that the survivors make a living catching insects in bamboo thickets and teak plantations.

Bumble-bee bats, like most bats, are beasts of mystery. As the species slithers towards extinction, no one really knows exactly what they eat, or how they find it. No one knows how they breed, or what sort of social life they lead. How can you sort out a proper conservation programme for an animal, when you don't even know where its food comes from? We are working in the dark, and are rather less suited to the task than bats.

Everywhere we turn in nature, we find that life is more diverse, more complicated than we believed possible. This is true for everyone who looks at nature: from the most casual observer to the greatest naturalist that ever drew breath. The more you look, the more extraordinary it gets. Which is why bumble-bee bats matter, of course.

14 Ivory-billed woodpecker

PATTERNS begin to emerge when you study conservation. An animal that likes plenty of space, and which lives close to humans, is likely to find itself on the endangered list. If the animal in question is big, and the kind of space it likes best is forest – well, it's almost as if the creature were asking for trouble.

This is true for large furry mammals; it is just as true for large birds. Small animals, like mice and tiny birds, have a terrific ability to recover. They can breed at a very fast rate when conditions are favourable. There are some animals, like the short-tailed field voles of Europe, that live in cycles of boom and bust. Sometimes there are lots of them; sometimes there are few. But as soon as things move in their favour – that is to say, more food around – they are right back to boom again. Suddenly, the population doubles and quadruples. The way the field voles live is designed for rapid recovery. Under normal circumstances, all disasters are small disasters, and can be dealt with.

This does not happen with large mammals, or large birds. They breed slowly, to maintain a stable, fixed population. This is all part of the package of being big. It takes time to for an elephant, or a blue whale, to develop inside its mother; likewise, big birds of prey can only produce and feed to adulthood one or two young a year. For big animals, there is no such thing as a small disaster.

And this is true of the **ivory-billed woodpecker**: a big woodpecker that needs huge areas of forest. Not just any forest, either: they need 'virgin forest' – that is to say, forest that has not been replanted, tidied and repeatedly felled by humans.

The terrible thing about the ivory-billed woodpeckers is that it might be too late. They are listed as endangered, possibly extinct. They lived, or they used to live, in south-eastern parts

IVORY-BILLED WOODPECKER
Scientific name: *Campephilus principalis*
Size: length up to 50 cm (19.5 in.)
Range: Cuba, USA
Habitat: mature swamp forest, pinewood, mixed forest
Food: beetle larvae found beneath bark

of the US and in Cuba. The last known nesting population in the US disappeared in 1948, when an area of Louisiana forest was cleared for growing beans. The last ivory-billed woodpecker in the US was seen in 1970.

They have hung on longer in Cuba; there were sightings in 1988, and a possible sighting in 1991. Since then, plenty of people have looked for the ivory-billed woodpecker, but no one has seen one. There is still suitable habitat left in Cuba. Sadly and oddly, the best bit of forest – apparently perfect for ivory-billed woodpeckers – has never been known to have any.

The smaller the population, the more vulnerable the animal. That seems obvious, I know. But it works like this: an animal is reduced to a small population for the various reasons we have already looked at in this book. It then discovers that smallness is itself a problem.

The ivory-billed woodpeckers were reduced to a single breeding population. That means that a single disaster can wipe them out. It may not always be a human–made disaster, like the destruction of the forest to grow beans. It may be a freeze, a hurricane, a disease, a fire. One disaster, a small disaster: and there is no recovery.

Once a population starts to go downhill, it goes faster and faster. That is the story of the ivory-billed woodpecker. There is no conservation programme for ivory-billed woodpeckers: how can there be, since no one is sure whether or not they still exist? It is possible that they will turn up again in the wild: a faint chance, but as we have seen with the kakapo and the megamouth shark, things do turn up. But the odds are against it: the odds have been against the ivory-billed woodpeckers as soon as people began to destroy their forests.

15 Blue whale

THE ivory-billed woodpecker's story is about the problem of size: it is a big bird, and it needs a lot of space. Let us now move on to the biggest animal that ever existed – not a dinosaur, but a whale.

The sight of a whale diving deep - sounding, they call it – is one of the most heartening things in the world. You can see little but a dark, rubbery back, curving down before you at a terrific rate. And then suddenly, the great flukes of the tail burst from the surface, and you cannot believe that one small part of an animal can be so colossal, towering above the seas for a brief and majestic second, before vanishing into the deep.

And you think that if the oceans can still hold a creature that strange – that *big* – then there is plenty of hope left for the world and its creatures.

And we are right to do so. There are many species of whale, and they are, like most large animals, in danger. But the fact that there are any left at all is enough to fill you up with hope. Conservation is a difficult matter, and sometimes a depressing one. But a single whale tells you that the struggle is worth it.

I have chosen the **blue whale** as the book's first whale for one simple reason: it is the biggest. The record is held by a female that measured 33.58 metres. We have talked about the slow speed at which large animals breed: a female blue whale gives birth to a young whale – they are called calves, oddly enough, since anything less like a calf would be hard to imagine – only once every two or three years. It takes whales an age to recover from a disaster, and the blue whales have been living through a disaster since the harpoon cannon was invented over a century ago.

Whales have been hunted for centuries, for their meat, their

BLUE WHALE
Scientific name: *Balaenoptera musculus*
Size: length up to 27 m (88 ft)
　　　weight up to 150 tons
Range: oceans of the world
Habitat: ocean
Food: krill (small shrimp-like animals)

whalebone, and the oil they have in their bodies. The invention of the harpoon cannon meant that the biggest and fastest whales could be hunted and killed. That put the blue whale right into the target area. The biggest: the best. And blue whales were hunted more than any other kind.

Whales are, of course, mammals, like us. They breathe the air: they communicate in strange sounds. They have large and complicated brains. We know very little about them and how they think. We do know that they are like us in many ways: but that did not stop the killing. In 1930, 30,000 blue whales were killed.

It has long been the nature of humans to believe that nature is a bottomless bucket, from which we can take what we want. No matter how much we take, the bucket will never grow empty. Trees, fish, bison, whales: plenty more where that came from.

But the case of the blue whale was one of the first where people realised that the supply was running out – before it actually did. The bucket was all but empty. For years, people predicted the extinction of the blue whale. In 1966, the whale was at last given protection, at a time when there were no more than a few hundred left.

The animals have begun to recover their numbers. That, again, is something to cheer about. It will be centuries before they have recovered to their full numbers, but conservationists should think like that. A century is but a moment in the history of a species. The blue whale, at least, is on the right road.

This means that soon people will be clamouring to hunt it again. It is inevitable. And these calls must be resisted. We don't know much about whales, how they communicate, how they live, but we do know exactly what over-hunting will do to them.

16 African elephant

WE have already had the Asian elephant, but I make absolutely no apology for bringing in another elephant. Why? I love them, simply enough. But then who doesn't?

African elephants are even bigger than Asian elephants. They are monsters: yet they love peace and quiet and company. They spend most of the day eating, quietly socialising, and occasionally playing. And practically everyone loves them. Elephants are just colossally lovable beasts.

People who write about nature, about extinction, about animals, try very hard to be clear, straightforward, and unemotional. This is true whether they are writing for the purpose of science or to prove a point for conservation. In both situations, only hard facts will do. If you don't have evidence for every single one of your facts, you will be in deep trouble. But the reason that people want to study the natural

world, and to save it, isn't entirely a matter of hard facts. There is also the question of love: love of fellow-animals, love of the wild. An American naturalist named Edward O. Wilson has called this 'biophilia', which means love of life. It is part of us. That is why we keep dogs and cats as pets, or a tank of fish. It is why we throw bread to ducks; it is also why we want to save the planet.

Biophilia: the sight of an elephant is enough to convince most of us that biophilia is a real thing: and an important thing. Throughout this book, I am constantly writing that humans killed this, destroyed that, as if humans were to blame for the current crisis: which we are. As if humans were the sworn enemies of every other living species on Earth: which we are not. Quite the opposite.

Biophilia is part of being human. Biophilia is something that links us to the other living things on this planet. Biophilia is why people take a walk in the countryside, or in the park: biophilia is why people go to the seaside for a holiday.

Everyone that ever patted a dog knows about biophilia. And it is time that people owned up to the fact. The wild world is part of us: and we are part of it. There are all kinds of good reasons for saving the planet: it is good for us, it is wise, it is our duty to other animals.

AFRICAN ELEPHANT
Scientific name: *Loxodonta africana*
Size: head and body length up to 25 ft (7.5 m)
height to shoulder up to 11.2 ft (3.4 m)
weight up to 13,892 lb (3,500 kg)
Range: Africa south of Sahara
Habitat: savannah, forest
Food: up to 300 species of plant

But the reason we *want* to save it is biophilia. Love. And the reason we may succeed comes down to the same thing. Love.

Which does not mean that the beloved African elephant is safe. In Africa, the problems caused by the human population are less great than in Asia. Africa is far less crowded: and the vast national parks which give the big animals of Africa a safe place to live were established before human populations could put them under the same kind of pressure they have in Asia.

But the world has a huge appetite for elephants' tusks. Perhaps this is a twisted example of biophilia. Ivory – the material from which a tusk is made – can be carved into beautiful things: but never half so beautiful as ivory on a living elephant. Male and female African elephants have tusks, only the male Asian elephants. And the African elephants have bigger tusks, too.

The trade in ivory used to be legal across the world. That meant that African elephants were killed, illegally, in the national parks, and their tusks smuggled out of the country. Then the trade was made illegal, and the poaching more or less stopped. There was no money in it. But in 1997, because the elephants had recovered, the trade was once again made legal. This was enough to make sure that the poaching started again.

This is painful for many of us. Not only because we *think* it is wrong; also because we *know* it is wrong. And the reason we feel so certain is biophilia. Biophilia: it is part of the human spirit.

17 Spix's macaw

THERE are times when conservation seems to be nothing less than a joke. The joke isn't exactly funny, but it's certainly absurd. And perhaps we can learn something from the absurdity of it all. Which brings me to the strange story of **Spix's macaw**, the animal that is ready to go extinct for a giggle.

As we have seen with the African wild dog and with all other animals that have been considered 'vermin', an animal is in a bad state if humans take a dislike to it. But an animal is not much better off if humans really like it. Humans really like Spix's macaw. And that liking has more or less done for it.

Humans have always liked parrots of all kinds; macaws are members of the parrot family. And humans like to keep them as pets. Parrots are sociable, intelligent, long-lived, good companions. But they are a lot of trouble to breed in captivity, and so many are taken from the wild every year. And as you will guess at once, we are back to the bottomless bucket principle.

'Plenty more parrots out there: so it doesn't make any difference if I take a few more, does it? And if I don't, somebody else will.' And so the trade in wild birds continues. There is an additional problem. The best way to catch parrots is to take the young ones from the nest, before they can fly. And the easiest way to reach a parrot's nest is not to climb the tree, but to chop the tree down. Parrots all over the world are caught in another of those human pincer movements. They are gathered up for the collectors and as they are gathered, their homes, their habitats are destroyed. The present generation is taken away, and there is nowhere for the future generation to go.

All parrot species suffer from this kind of problem. They are too well loved by humans to lead a safe life. But with Spix's macaw, matters have reached the level of a grim and horrible joke.

There came a point when there was only one Spix's macaw left out in the wild. These macaws were never very common. They lived only in the trees around a river in Brazil, the São Francisco. Many of the trees were cut for firewood: collection mania did for most of the rest.

There is still a small population of Spix's macaws left in captivity, and the Brazilian government set up a programme to try and bring the bird back from the brink. By 1995, the captive population had gone up, with seven new birds, thanks to successful efforts to breed the captive macaws. Meanwhile, the wild population went up by one: one of the captive birds was released back into the wild to keep the lone bird company. A female was released to go out there and join the male. Of course, everybody hoped they would get together and breed.

The trouble was, the one wild Spix's macaw had been living with a bird of the wrong species, a blue-winged macaw. Obviously, the pair could not mate: but parrots love companionship, and they stuck together. The situation is crazy: it's almost, but not quite, funny. Later on, the female Spix disappeared, and the male stayed with his blue-winged macaw. The next plan is to give the pair a couple of real Spix's eggs from the captive population. Perhaps the mixed pair of macaws can between them rear a real wild Spix.

I know this all seems deeply mad, and so it is. But the real craziness came from all that went before: the forest destruction, and in particular, the collection mania. Compared to everything that brought Spix's macaw to the brink of extinction, the crazy scenes along the São Francisco River represent sanity. They show a kind of hope and, in a world full of problems, the only true sanity lies in hope.

SPIX'S MACAW
Scientific name: *Cyanopsitta spixii*
Size: length up to 56 cm (22 in.)
Range: Brazil
Habitat: gallery woodland with caraiba trees
Food: seeds, fruit

18 Australian ant

ELEPHANTS are easy to love. Biophilia is the easiest thing in the world to understand when you are looking at an elephant. So let us now consider ants. On the face of it, these are very hard creatures to love.

Cuddling is not the only way of loving, however. And there are people in this world who are passionate about ants: and eager to share their passion with the rest of us. Let us start with biodiversity: there are about 9,500 species of ants known to science and perhaps three times that number still waiting to be discovered. There are great differences, great areas of diversity between all these species. The world's smallest ant could live comfortably inside the braincase of the world's largest ant.

How many individual ants are there in the world? There is an estimate of one million billion. It is impossible even to begin to understand so colossal a number: it is like trying to count the stars on a frosty night, or the grains of sand on a beach. The ants of this planet weigh as much as all the human beings put together. In the rainforest, the total weight of ants, wasps, bees and termites adds up to one third of the weight of all animal species. They probably add up to a still bigger fraction of the weight of animals in the desert. People say that we live in the age of mammals; or the age of humankind. But we live in the age of ants.

Ants have lived in the world from the time of the dinosaurs. They have existed more than 50 times longer than the entire history of humans. Such huge numbers, so long a history. What makes ants so successful? The answer is simple and immensely complicated at the same time. For the answer is sharing. Working together. Co-operation.

The ants have brought the art of living together to the highest

possible level. Every ant in a colony is the offspring of a single mother, the queen. Ants regularly commit suicide for the sake of the colony. They farm other creatures, the aphids; they farm their own crops of fungus. Ants are endlessly complicated, endlessly baffling, endlessly fascinating. And for the most part endlessly successful. Ants are probably better equipped to withstand major catastrophes than humans. For a start, they have been at it for longer.

But all the same, there are species of ants that are in danger: and I have chosen the **Australian ant** to represent them all. The species, also known as the dinosaur ant, is found only in an area of South Australia, a tiny chunk of land, not much more than a square kilometre. The ants live in tall eucalyptus woodland, where the leaves overhead form a closed roof, or canopy. They live in underground nests and emerge at night to hunt for other species of insect.

The species was first discovered in 1934, but the only living colonies were discovered many years later, in 1977. These were destroyed when an underground telephone cable was laid; but since then, three more sites have been discovered close by. The humans living near by have been helpful in conservation, but the area is heavily populated, which means that a full-blown conservation plan cannot be set up. The species remains extremely vulnerable. A single bush-fire could wipe them out. The best hope for the animals is hope itself: the hope that there are further colonies of these ants that haven't yet been discovered. If so, a proper conservation plan can be set up.

Ants are disturbing, slightly spooky animals: that is why those who love ants love them very much. Our large brains and clever hands are not the only reasons that humans became so dominant a species on this planet. It's also because of our ability to co-operate: to share our work, our food, our shelter. That is why ants always make humans feel uneasy and humble. Ants survive and, mostly, prosper, for exactly the same reasons as we do. The difference is that they are much better at it than us.

AUSTRALIAN ANT
Scientific name: *Nothomyrmecia macrops*
Size: workers about 1 cm (0.4 in.)
Range: Australia
Habitat: eucalyptus woodland
Food: insects

19 Seychelles magpie-robin

AS we march on through the book, species by species, we should, perhaps, pause for breath. What is a species? It's obvious; and then again, it's not obvious. A willow warbler and a chiffchaff: two little green birds that look almost identical. Even a good birdwatcher sometimes finds it impossible to tell them apart. But they live different lives, sing different songs, go to different places to spend their winters. And if you put a willow warbler and a chiffchaff together, they will not produce a nest full of baby willow-chiffs.

A Great Dane and a dachshund are dogs that look so unalike that it seems impossible that they could be the same species. But they are both dogs: and indeed, there have been cross-breed Great Dane/dachshunds. A white-skinned human can look very different from a black-skinned human, but all humans are the same species. We can, and do, breed across different races and cultures.

It is a fact that humans beings are more closely related to chimpanzees than willow warblers are to chiffchaffs. But humans cannot breed with chimpanzees. The very thought is disturbing. The notion of a human cross-breeding with some other kind of animal makes up many of our ancient myths and modern horror-stories.

The thought is disturbing, not only because it seems unnatural, but because it *is* unnatural. The idea of species is important, not just to humans, but to the entire natural world. Humans like to organise nature into boxes as a way of understanding nature's vastness. It cannot be denied that these are very helpful devices; but the only box that really matters is species.

Once, people believed that a species of animal was fixed for all time. A species had always existed: and would always exist.

SEYCHELLES MAGPIE-ROBIN

Scientific name: *Copsychus sechellarum*
Size: head and body length 25 cm (9.9 in.)
Range: Seychelles
Habitat: breadfruit groves, cashew plantations,
coffee and vegetable gardens
Food: invertebrates, small lizards, fruit

Now we know this is not true. The dinosaurs came to an end: many of the animals alive today will come to an end soon, if we do not do something about it.

New species came into existence after the dinosaurs had gone. How does a new species come about? This is perhaps the mystery of mysteries. But if we seek to understand the mystery, the best place to start looking is an island.

A species comes to an island by chance, and finds a way of making a living. If things work well, a new population is established on the island. But the differences between the island and the place from which the animal has come, and the fact that the animal has no contact with the members of its species that got left behind means that changes begin to take place. The island population changes, sometimes drastically. It has gone past the point of no return. It is a new and separate species.

That is why, all over the world, there are islands that contain species that are not found anywhere else. The animals have claimed the island, and also, the island has claimed them. This happens most noticeably with birds.

Just such a bird is the **Seychelles magpie-robin**. There are eight species of magpie-robin living in Africa and Asia: dapper, perky little birds. In years gone by, a few members of one of these species made their way to the Seychelles, and over the years, a new species was established. The Seychelles magpie-robin is out on its own, a totally separate species. It feeds on worms and insects, and delights in following tortoises and pigs, eating the insects disturbed by the big animals as they pass.

At one stage, the Seychelles magpie-robin was down to 15 individuals. We know how vulnerable a small population can be – a single disaster can wipe it out. An island species is, almost by definition, a small population. It takes a very small amount of human clumsiness to create a disaster.

Forest clearing began almost as soon as humans arrived in the Seychelles in 1770; and in little more than 100 years, the Seychelles magpie-robin was extinct in the largest island in the Seychelles, Mahe. Habitat destruction, and the introduction of cats and rats – a pretty familiar story already, this one – continued to destroy the magpie-robin population. Further extinctions followed. But the bird hung on on a single island, Fregate.

Eventually, international efforts for the conservation of this bird began in earnest. Magpie-robins have been reintroduced to Aride. There has been work on habitat, including the replanting of native trees. Cats have been controlled. In other words, people have tried to recreate the habitat that their predecessors destroyed. There are now hopes of getting the magpie-robin population back up to the 100-mark.

Such a population is still horribly vulnerable, of course, which is all the more reason to look after it. The notion of an island species, set about by a sea of troubles, is one to which we shall return more than once. We shall do so with the story of the Seychelles magpie-robin in mind. It is a story of – cautious – hope.

20 Lake Victoria cichlids

THERE is another twist to the story of island species. The original animals arriving on an island often form a species quite distinct from their ancestors, as we have seen with the Seychelles magpie-robin. But sometimes they go on to form more than one species. From one species of animal, several, sometimes many, different species come into being, and often in a very short period of time. Islands represent evolution on fast-forward.

The most famous example of this is Darwin's finches, on the Galapagos islands. The ancestors of these little birds were a single species, doubtless blown in from South America. From this one species have come 13 species of finch, each living in a different way. There were no woodpeckers on the Galapagos islands, so a finch took on the job of hunting insects in tree-trunks. Some finches have slender bills and eat insects and drink nectar. Other have thick bills to tear apart fruit and seeds. Others – vampire finches, they are called, sinister name for a sinister lifestyle – drink the blood of large seabirds, and also eat their eggs.

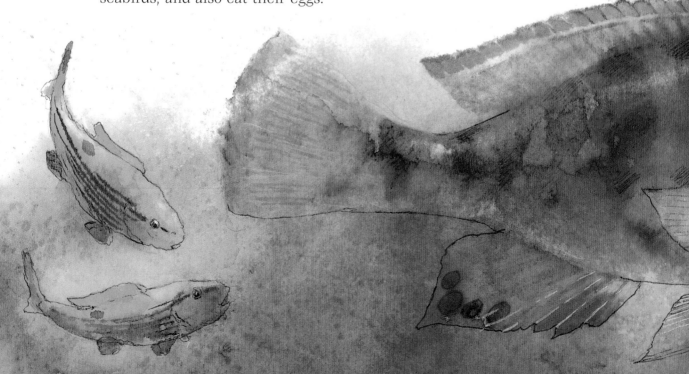

Such strange populations of unique birds are an aspect of island life. But for my next beast, I will take an island that is not a speck of land in a vast area of water: but a cut-off area of water in a vast mass of land. This is Lake Victoria in Africa. Like the Seychelles, like the Galapagos islands, it is a place in which the animals are cut off from other populations.

Galapagos has 13 species of finch. Lake Victoria has – or had – 300 species of cichlids. These **Lake Victoria cichlids** are fish. If you think we had better name, for the sake of it, one single species to represent all the rest of this vast and varied collection, let us choose, at random, the charming-looking **Paralabidochromis chilotes**, a heavy-lipped cichlid that feeds on insects. You must excuse the scientific name; the fish are mysterious things, not widely known as individual species to anyone except scientists, and so they do not have English-language names.

It seems that these 300 species of fish all came from a single ancestral species. They have radiated out from this, in all manner of shapes and sizes, to find just about every way in which it is possible for a fish to make a living. This makes Lake Victoria one of the most extraordinary and mysterious places on Earth.

Islands are fragile places, and island species are fragile groups. This is true whether the island is land or water. A very small act of human interference is often a disaster, and so it was with Lake

LAKE VICTORIA CICHLID
Scientific name: All Lake Victoria cichlids
    from the family Cichlidae, chosen species
    Paralabidochromis chilotes
Size: few longer than 30 cm (12 in.)
Range: Lake Victoria (Kenya, Tanzania, Uganda)
Habitat: Lake Victoria
Food: different species have different foods,
    including fish, insects, crustaceans, molluscs,
    algae, plankton

Victoria. Someone decided that it would be good idea to fill the lake with a kind of fish that was fun to catch and good to eat: the Nile perch.

Once again, the goalposts of evolution were moved. The cichlid species had grown up to be very good at their various different ways of life – which did not include escaping from Nile perch. And so the Nile perch started to clean up. They ate individuals; they ate entire species. The introduction of exotic species is, after habitat destruction, the biggest cause of extinction in the current and terrible extinction event that is unfolding before us. The fact of the matter is that nature is so big and so complex that you cannot predict it. You simply cannot tell what an introduced species will do. No one can.

The Nile perch has already done terrible damage to the Lake Victoria cichlids. But there are other problems. Before the Nile perch were introduced, people had fished the waters too heavily, on the old and terrible argument that if they didn't kill the fish, someone else would. The lake is also polluted, and short of oxygen.

How many of these cichlids have already gone? It is estimated that as many 200 of the 300 species have disappeared. Now what?

There are currently 30 species being reared in aquariums. The long-term plan is for re-release into the wild. The three countries that border the lake, Kenya, Tanzania and Uganda, have signed an agreement with a long-term view of managing the lake more sympathetically. It is a start. It is too late for the 200 species that have gone. But not too late to give up hope for the rest.

21 Sokoke scops owl

I WOULD never have found them myself, but I was with a man who knew and understood his forest. And his owls. Owls hunt mostly at night. During the daylight hours they find somewhere safe and secret to hide away, waiting for darkness so that hunting can begin again. The places are called day-roosts, and I found I was looking, through a tunnel of undergrowth, at just such a day-roost. There were two owls, so close as to be almost cuddling, one ashy grey, one bright tangerine (the species varies in colour from individual to individual). Almost like toy owls, because they were tiny, sitting upright like sentries, no taller than 15 centimetres. And, as is the way of owls, they looked very cross but very cuddly at the same time.

Actually, they were probably just a little frightened. So we moved no closer; and after a moment, slipped away. I had just seen the world's rarest owl: the **Sokoke scops owl**.

It is another island species – of a kind, anyway. The island is not in the middle of the sea, however: it is in the vast continent of Africa. The island is a strip of forest near the coast of Kenya. It does not look terribly special. But it is: an island of forest in the middle of a quite different habitat. The Arabuko-Sokoke forest is the home for this tiny and more or less unique owl. It was not discovered until 1965, and was only known to live in the Sokoke forest. However, in 1992, a single Sokoke scops owl was found miles away in Tanzania – so it is possible that there are more of them about than was first thought, which is encouraging.

This little island of forest has other creatures that live only in Sokoke. There are another five species of endangered bird: Clarke's weaver, East coast akalat, Sokoke pipit, spotted ground thrush and Amani sunbird. There are also mammals that live only in this odd

SOKOKE SCOPS OWL
Scientific name: *Otus ireneae*
Size: head and body length up to 18 cm (7 in.)
weight up to 50 g (1.8 oz)
Range: Kenya
Habitat: forest
Food: large insects

little forest: a tiny deer, Ader's duiker, the Sokoke bushy-tailed mongoose, and the golden-rumped elephant shrew. Island rules apply to this island of forest: the animals inside it are cut off from other populations. They become specialised to the life of their own small area. And they become, over a long period of time, separate species. The Arabuko-Sokoke forest is a startlingly rich place. It is a hotspot of biodiversity: a place where a number of unique species are clustered together.

Such special places need special cherishing. But the Arabuko-Sokoke forest has always been a working forest. People have always used it for the gathering of firewood and the collection of fruit and plants for medicine.

The one way you cannot protect such a forest is to ban people from it. You would need hundreds of armed guards, night and day. And you would encounter nothing but hostility: and rightly so. The conservation effort in the Arabuko-Sokoke forest is one of the many that seeks to work alongside people, rather than against them, to maintain the forest as an important asset for local people. Increasingly, tourists come to the forest to see its unique animals. The idea is to create a source not only of pride, but of money for the people who live around the forest.

It is a delicate and ticklish thing to do: but the Arabuko-Sokoke project is designed to be a model of its kind. Just as an island is a kind of model for those who study animals and their evolution and biodiversity, so a good, small-scale conservation project can and should become a model for good conservation. The lessons of an island can be taken on and applied to the greater world.

22 Yangtze river dolphin

EVERYBODY knows about dolphins: the great show-offs of the open oceans. And dolphins have always been sailors' favourite animals, too. They follow ships, ride the bow-wave like surfers, leap and play close by. Sailors have always liked them.

As more is known about them, so they have become favourite animals of people who have never been to sea, never been on a boat. For there is something in dolphins that humans relate to. They are intelligent animals, with complex brains. They are fishy creatures, but with something of a human face: a bright eye, and a mouth that seems to be curved in a smile. And like us, they are of course mammals. They breathe the air. Like us, but unlike fish, a dolphin can drown.

Like us, dolphins love light and air and good company. But there are many different species of dolphin, and some of them live dramatically different lives from the leapers and plungers of the open ocean. There are about 45 species of dolphin altogether: once again, we find the wonders of biodiversity.

And where we find biodiversity, we tend also to find specialists: animals that have adapted beautifully for a certain specialised way of life. Specialisation is always a fascinating development, and potentially a very dangerous one. Some call it the Tender Trap.

YANGTZE RIVER DOLPHIN
Scientific name: *Lipotes vexillifer*
Size: length up to 2.4 m (8 ft)
weight up to 80 kg (180 lb)
Range: China
Habitat: River Yangtze
Food: fish, freshwater shrimps

Dolphins, animals of the salty oceans, moved into the great river systems of the world. Over the course of the years, these river dolphins changed to become specialists with a very different way of making a living to that of the ocean-dwellers. There are five species of river dolphin, all in various kinds of danger because of the Tender Trap. And the one in the greatest danger is the **Yangtze river dolphin**, which also has the Chinese name of *baiji*.

The other species of river dolphin live in the Amazon, the Plate, the Indus and the Ganges. Each is unique, but has specialised in a similar way to the others. The Yangtze river dolphin lives in the perpetual murk of a muddy river, and can hardly see at all. There are probably no more than 300 of them left.

The Yangtze river dolphin finds its way around, and it finds its prey – fish, and probably shrimps – by sonar. That is to say, it makes a noise, and listens to the echo, using these reflected sounds to make a picture of its environment. It can, if you like, see with its ears. It has a long thin beak, which does not fit our ideas of what a dolphin should look like. It probably uses it for digging in the mud after shrimps. I say probably, because no one has watched one. How can you watch an animal in liquid mud? These will always be animals of mystery.

And here is where the Tender Trap comes in. The Yangtze river dolphin has adapted perfectly for its environment, which is the river Yangtze. This makes them, in effect, another island species: they are cut off from the rest of their kind, they have gone their own way, and

there is no going back. They have specialised in their environment of fresh water and mud and perpetual dark. The open oceans are a foreign place to them. They are trapped in their river, by their own skills in adapting to it. And if you change the river, the dolphins cannot change with it.

The Yangtze runs through the middle of China, the most populous nation on Earth. The Yangtze is more than a home for dolphins – it is also a larder for fish-eating people, a highway for their boats. It is also a running tap for watering crops, and a generator, because its flow is used for making electricity.

Dolphins get damaged by boats, especially the whirring propellers, and by fishing gear. They can drown in fishing nets. The more people who use the river, the more difficult it is for dolphins to live the life they have adapted for. Once again the goalposts of evolution have been moved.

However, the Chinese are fond of their mysterious dolphins, and in that fact lies their greatest hope. The city of Tongling has adopted the animal as a mascot. There is even a local baiji beer named after it. The first reserve for dolphins opened there recently, with the aim of establishing a semi-wild breeding population.

More such reserves are needed. More important still, the dolphins need safe areas of river. Another small but important step would be the fitting of guards around the propellers of boats. But at least the conservation effort is off to a good start.

23 Rockhopper penguin

THE biggest and wildest island left on Earth is the island continent of the Antarctic. You cannot tell where the land ends and the sea begins, because both are covered with ice. In the coldest times of the year, the sheet of ice extends 1,000 kilometres from the shore into the sea.

It was the last place on Earth where animals were left undisturbed. The penguins and seals that used the land had the place to themselves, along with the flying seabirds. Why would any animal choose to live in so cold, so difficult a place? Because there is food. When there is food, be sure that some kind of animal will come in and eat it. That is how nature works.

There is very good fishing to be had in the world's coldest seas, starting with huge and incomprehensible numbers of the tiny shrimp-like creatures called krill. These bring in the giant whales, the blue whale being the biggest of them all.

Humans have also been coming to the southern oceans for years. Many came to hunt, and not only for food. They came close to hunting various species of seals to extinction, and also, as we have seen, the great whales. The numbers of both kinds of animals are increasing again, but it is a delicate situation and one that needs constant watching.

More recently, humans have started to explore the land of the Antarctic in search of oil and minerals. The pollution from any major industry would be a disaster for the Antarctic – worse than in most other places on Earth. It is so difficult for any kind of animal to live there, that a small amount of trouble, a small amount of disturbance and pollution, goes a very long way.

The animal I choose to represent the Antarctic on this book's first

ROCKHOPPER PENGUIN

Scientific name: *Eudyptes chrysocome*
Size: length 55 cm (21 in.)
Range: sub-Antarctic oceans, sub-Antarctic islands
Habitat: ocean; come to cliffs to nest
Food: fish, squid

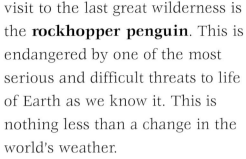

visit to the last great wilderness is the **rockhopper penguin**. This is endangered by one of the most serious and difficult threats to life of Earth as we know it. This is nothing less than a change in the world's weather.

The world is getting warmer. Human industries and the human way of life – our cars, the way we heat our homes – put gases into the air. These gases allow the heat of the sun through the atmosphere but trap it, once it is in. This is how a greenhouse works, and the gases that cause it are called greenhouse gases.

The greenhouse effect is felt most strongly in the coldest part of the world. You might think that the Antarctic would welcome a bit of warmth, but that is not the way it works. The Wordie ice-sheet, a colossal area the size of the country of Luxembourg, has disintegrated as the temperature has risen by 2.5 degrees on the Antarctic peninsula.

This happens to be a place where the rockhopper penguins nest. The break-up of their home means that they have fewer and fewer places to go. In some places, the numbers of rockhoppers are down 90 per cent.

It is a huge and difficult problem. The birds at the bottom of the planet are suffering because of problem created right at the top of the planet – for it is in the north that most of the greenhouse gases are sent up into the atmosphere.

Penguins are wonderful birds, both comic and brilliant. They have abandoned flight and become the best swimmers of bird-kind. The rockhoppers spend the long winters out to sea, but come together in what were once huge social gatherings in order to breed. They line up in giant mixed colonies with black-browed albatross and king shag, other birds of the southern oceans.

The world is only just beginning to understand that global warming is serious. To those of us who live in cold climates it seems a joke, rather a nice idea. But it is changing the way in which the weather of the world operates. Once again, humans are moving the goalposts of evolution.

24 Polar bear

FROM the land at the bottom of the Earth to the very top, and the Arctic. No island, this: the Arctic is not a single continent, like the Antarctic. It is made up of the top part of the three northern continents, a few islands, and a great deal of frozen sea.

It is surrounded by human population, human pressure, human industries, human invasions. There is plenty of the Arctic that is wild: but it is completely encircled by people. Like every other wild place left on Earth, the Arctic is an island of wilderness surrounded by humans. It is hard to get wilder than the frozen north: but here, as everywhere, wilderness feels the pressure of people.

There is no better animal to stand for the great white North than the **polar bear**. Polar bears can be found all round the Arctic, in the very northernmost parts of North America, Europe, Asia, Greenland and Spitsbergen.

Polar bears are huge and fierce, and that is something that makes them especially vulnerable, as we have already seen with the tiger. Polar bears must be considered as another kind of island animal, and that makes them still more vulnerable.

Polar bears eat mainly seals, though they have been known to eat small whales as well. They are powerful swimmers. The role of top carnivore in a vast place with very few animals in it is a very difficult one, but the polar bear manages it with some ease, for it is a truly remarkable animal.

The Arctic is not a single island-continent like the Antarctic at the other end of the world. The Arctic Circle includes bits of America, Europe and Asia. The Arctic is connected to all the great land-masses of Earth. For that reason, it has been available for tough-minded people for centuries. The polar bear has been hunted by them, for its meat, and for its fur. But the pace hotted up when Europeans came in, and hunted for sport and for furs to sell, rather than to wear.

In 1973, the countries that had polar bears agreed to stop outsiders hunting for sport or for business. Local people like the Inuit were permitted to kill a certain number of bears annually, to maintain their traditional ways of life. But how can you police so vast an area? Poachers come in and the animal is still very vulnerable.

But that is not the worst of it. The Arctic is now a place for oil-drilling, and for digging for minerals. The rich fishing around the area naturally brings in fishing boats, and the fishermen take too many fish. They know that if they don't, someone else will. Increasingly, the shortage of fish affects the numbers of seals, and that in turn affects the number of polar bears.

It is very hard indeed for life to hang on in so cold and so problematic a place. Small amounts of disturbance and pollution have very great effects. And we do not need to imagine the effects of a great amount of pollution, because in 1989, a supertanker called

POLAR BEAR
Scientific name: *Ursus maritimus*
Size: head and body up to 2.5 m (8 ft)
weight up to 800 kg (1,764 lb)
Range: Arctic
Habitat: Arctic waters, icecaps, land
Food: mainly seals, also fish, vegetable matter
in summer

the Exxon Valdez ran aground in the Arctic, off the coast of Alaska. It was carrying 50 million tonnes of crude oil. This formed an oil slick that covered 800 kilometres of coast. It killed 32,000 birds, 950 sea otters, and untold millions of fish. All life is affected by such a disaster: and those that feel it most, if indirectly, are the top predators. In the Arctic, that means the polar bears.

There are new roads being built in the Arctic, and new airports, and these bring in more and more people who come also for tourism and for hunting. All these things cause disturbance and pollution: some Arctic countries are better than others at cleaning up.

The Arctic is a vast place, but it is most extraordinarily delicate. Life on the margins is always difficult, and polar bears live on the very edge of what is possible. It is hard for people to come to terms with the fact that places so huge can also be so fragile. Human clumsiness can do as much damage as deliberate destruction.

25 Black rhinoceros

IN Tanzania, in Africa, there is a walled and circular garden. The wall was created when a volcano erupted and collapsed. It is a called the Ngorongoro Crater, and it is one of the wonders of the world.

The crater holds permanent water, and water is one of the keys to life. For this reason, it has always held extraordinary numbers of animals for its size: the place is rich, and freakish. To reach it, you drive across a lot of rather bare country where the only animals you see are domestic cattle, a few gazelles, a few ostrich.

But the crater heaves with life. Elephant, buffalo, wildebeest, lion. The place is a natural island of wildlife. And it also holds another animal: the **black rhinoceros**. The reason for this is not the permanent water, but the permanent wall. There are only a couple of safe routes down the steep wall of the crater. And once there, you can be easily spotted. If you were up to no good, it would be very hard to get into the crater without being seen – and almost impossible to get away without being caught.

And for that simple reason, the Ngorongoro Crater is the best place in the world to see black rhinos. They are the only black rhinos in the world that trust human beings. They actually feel safe in the presence of people.

A brief note before we carry on: black rhinos are not black. There is another animal called the white rhinoceros: this is not white. All five species of rhinoceros are grey, elephant-coloured, and like elephants, they take on the colour of the country they live in, because they love to roll in the dust.

One of the odd things about the black rhinoceros is that it

has no problem with habitat destruction. Since habitat destruction is one of the themes of this book, and one of the themes of the great episode of extinction, this idea takes a bit of getting used to. In places like the Luangwa Valley in Zambia, you can walk for miles through perfect, unspoiled black rhino country. But there are no black rhinos.

The black rhinos still exist in pockets and islands of country where the habitat is too difficult for easy hunting, the population too spread out, or the policing too efficient. Elsewhere, they have mostly been killed. A dead rhino is simply too valuable.

You can sell the horn of a rhino – any of the five species – for a very great deal of money. Rhino horn is a traditional and important ingredient in Chinese medicine. The horn is also used in Yemen, to make dagger handles. Possession of a rhino-horn dagger is considered a great thing, just as some Westerners love to have a flashy car or a specially expensive watch.

One of the problems of conservation – perhaps the greatest problem of them all – is that some countries are very rich, and others are very poor. And it is the poor countries that mostly have the best wildlife. If the rich people want something from the world's wildlife, all they have to do is fix a price.

BLACK RHINOCEROS
Scientific name: *Diceros bicornis*
Size: head and body up to 3.5 m (12.3 ft)
       height at shoulder up to 1.8 m (5.9 ft)
       weight up to 1,400 kg (3,087 lb)
Range: sub-Saharan Africa
Habitat: savannah
Food: leaves, grass

With the growing prosperity of some Chinese businesses, and of course the traditional prosperity of many of the Chinese who live in other countries of the world, there is a growing number of people who can afford the most expensive ingredients in traditional Chinese medicine. Like rhino horn. And as the oil industry made many people in Yemen rich, so many more people than before can afford rhino-horn daggers. The result has been the hunting of rhinos to the edge of extinction.

Trade in rhino horn is illegal all over the world, more or less, but when the money offered is so much, the law is regularly broken. Only in places like Ngorongoro Crater are the rhinos safe.

The black rhino is an impressive animal and, for that reason, it has naturally attracted a lot of conservation efforts. But mere policing is never going to stop a profitable trade. Tough laws have not stopped the trade in drugs, or in guns: they merely make them more expensive. The same is true with much of the wildlife trade, which, after the other two mentioned, is the third largest illegal trade in the world.

Efforts are being made to encourage people in Chinese medicine to turn to other ingredients. This is a slow business, but it has begun. In Yemen, other materials have been used in place of rhino horn, and are beginning to find favour. Back in Africa, we return once again to the question of involving local people in conservation. In bald terms, that means making a live rhino more valuable than a dead one. Good, non-polluting tourism is one of the best hopes for the future of the black rhino.

The best news of all is the habitat. If ever the world suddenly stops wanting to kill rhinos for their horn, there are still wonderful places for them to live. With the black rhino, there is no Humpty Dumpty Effect. The black rhino's case is almost unique in the fact that everything really could be put right tomorrow. But it will be a long time before that tomorrow comes around.

26 *Wandering albatross*

THE 'islands' in this book are getting bigger all the time. We have moved from the tiny specks of the Seychelles to the wildernesses of the poles. We have moved on to the great open spaces of Africa: places that seem endless, but which are under the same threat as any other island. So let's take the one last step and consider the wildest animal on Earth: the **wandering albatross**.

It is a strange thing, to see an albatross. The bird seems to be all wing. The wandering albatross has the longest wings of all the albatrosses, and therefore the longest wings in the world. Wing-tip to wing-tip, they are not much short of four metres.

The bird looks impossible: too much wing for a single bird to carry. And when you see one trying to take off, it looks even more impossible. On land they need long runways, and they charge along them until they have got enough speed to fly. At sea, they must patter along the surface for ages until they get going. They look foolish, rather comic.

But once they get going – then it is a different story. They are not much for flapping, but they are the greatest gliding animals that nature has ever produced. Down in the southern oceans where the wind never stops, they ride the air with stiff, endless wings. And they can cover unbelievable distances: 1,000 kilometres in a day is nothing to them.

The wandering albatross lives further from people than any other animal in existence. It is the most wild, the most free. Its home is the living air, the open ocean.

But even an albatross needs somewhere to lay an egg. The parent birds seek out the rocky islands that stick up out of the southern oceans and there, in big, noisy, rather quarrelsome colonies, they

WANDERING ALBATROSS
Scientific name: *Diomedea exulans*
Size: wing span up to 351 cm (138 in.)
   length up to 135 cm (53 in.)
Range: southern oceans, breeds on islands
Habitat: ocean
Food: fish, squid

raise a single chick. It takes, by bird standards, an extraordinary length of time: about nine months. When at last it is done, the chick, like an independent teenager, sets off to seek its fortune. It spends seven years at sea: flying, feeding, growing up.

Its parents part and go their separate ways. But 18 months later, they meet up at the same island, and the same pair will raise another chick. It is leisurely business, but the point is that albatrosses are very long-lived. They often survive into their thirties. Their entire, slow-motion breeding depends on them living a long time.

But even here, out in the wildest places on Earth, there is trouble. A wandering albatross lives as free from land as it is possible for an animal to do. And yet they too find problems. For them, the wildest place on Earth – the vast ocean – is no more than an island, surrounded by trouble.

The principal problem is fishing. Fishermen work the southern oceans for tuna. The blue-finned tuna is called 'the Porsche of the southern seas', partly because it swims very fast, and partly because, once caught, it is worth as much as a Porsche.

Fishermen catch tuna by throwing a series of hooks off the back of a boat, every few metres, on lines 100 kilometres long. To each hook they fix a piece of fish or squid. An albatross comes cruising in for a free meal, grabs a piece of bait – gets stuck on the hook and drowns.

Albatrosses can be kept away from the boat by using long streamers, which work on the same principle as the scarecrow. There are busy campaigns in Australia and elsewhere to persuade the fishing

fleets of the world to use the streamers. But they are difficult to operate properly, and in the midst of difficult and dangerous work, who can be bothered with such things?

As ever, we are talking about starts; as ever, we are working on the very edge of too late. The wandering albatross may be the world's greatest wanderer: but it can never wander far enough. It can never break free. It might just as well be living on a tiny speck of the world, like the Seychelles magpie-robin. All the animals in this book are, in their way, island species: surrounded, as I say, by troubles. And by now, we know where all the troubles come from.

27 Estuarine or saltwater crocodile

THERE is something particularly frightening about crocodiles. Lions, elephants, rhinoceroses, hippopotamuses: these are big and sometimes very dangerous animals. But they are not so plain terrifying as crocodiles.

Crocodiles are probably the most alarming animals that walk on the Earth today. Alarming to humans, I mean. Humans, like lions and the rest of the big animals I just mentioned, are mammals. We may be frightened by lions, we may even be killed by them – but at least we feel we can understand them. We understand something of their daily lives: their need to eat more or less every day, their need for companionship, the care of their young ones, the leadership. They are like us, warm-blooded. The rhythms of our different lives are not all that far apart.

But a crocodile is a reptile. It is cold-blooded, and it lives its life to a different rhythm. There is a very small river in Africa full of very large crocodiles. They eat just once a year. For just a few weeks of the year, the wildebeest, big grazing animals forever on the move, live near the river, and must drink there every day. For these few weeks, the crocodiles are busy: hunting, and above all, eating.
And for the rest of the entire year, they are quiet.

And as the year passes, they get hungrier and hungrier. A few weeks before the wildebeest arrive, the crocs are getting restless. They move about impatiently. They abandon their usual state of quiet rest. If you stand near the bank, they

ESTUARINE OR SALTWATER CROCODILE
Scientific name: *Crocodylus porosus*
Size: length up to 7 m (23 ft)
weight up to (sometimes over) 900 kg (2,000 lb)
Range: Australia, Indonesia, Papua New Guinea,
Asia from India eastward
Habitat: coastal brackish waters, tidal rivers
Food: young take crustaceans, insects, small fish;
adults take snakes, birds, turtles, cattle, horses,
occasionally humans

watch you, thinking, perhaps, about a charge out of the water: willing you, perhaps, to take a few steps closer, to take a drink. And sometimes they growl: a strange, unmammal-like crocodile's growl. It is perhaps the spookiest sound I have ever heard.

It is like being on another planet: or to be more accurate, like being back in another age. The first crocodiles appeared during the Age of the Dinosaurs. To visit crocodiles is to return to the Jurassic, millions of years before humans walked the Earth. Sometimes, elsewhere in Africa, crocodiles gather during the dry season in groups of one hundred at a time. The sight is the nearest a human can get to Jurassic Park.

All this is enough to make a human feel very weak and feeble. To stand close to the huge crocodiles is to feel completely powerless. They are alien monsters, long-term survivors. A human feels very small and insignificant, when faced with an animal six metres long and trailing 65 million years of history.

We are indeed a weak as well as a new-fangled species. Human against crocodile doesn't seem much of a contest. But the fact is that humans are the most powerful species on this planet. There is nothing humans cannot do. Or to put it another way, there is nothing that humans cannot destroy. No: not much of a contest. The human is going to win every time.

One species of crocodile in the middle of losing the contest is the **estuarine crocodile**, sometimes called the **saltwater crocodile**. This is the world's most widespread croc, found in Asia, Papua New Guinea and Australia. They like the places where rivers and sea meet: the brackish (salty) waters of coastal lagoons and estuaries.

They are impressive animals: big, sleek and fierce. But humans have power over them, as they do over every other species. The crocodiles have been caught in yet another human pincer movement. In the 1950s and 1960s, many estuarine crocs were killed for their skins, for the leather industry. The big crocs were targeted by the hunters (because they have more skin and therefore more leather) and this – since the big animals are the most experienced and therefore the most successful breeders – drastically reduced the breeding population.

Then came the second part of the pincer movement: habitat loss, with coastal lagoons and mangrove swamps cleared and drained for farming. Thus the chances of crocodiles recovering from the hunting were seriously affected because there were fewer and fewer places for them to live and breed.

There are now programmes for their conservation, and the most successful so far has been in India, where estuarine crocodiles have been released back into the wild, and have begun to breed. But as ever in these matters, humans have very great power indeed when it comes to destroying. When it comes to putting it all back together again – the Humpty Dumpty Effect – we discover that we are less powerful than we thought. Destruction, it seems, is what we do best. It is time to change that.

28 Takahe

WE tend to think of human power as a fairly recent thing. Most people believe that humans were not really powerful until farming methods changed so dramatically a couple of hundred years ago; or when factories and the great processes of industry began; or when the most fearsome weapons of war were developed; or when the human population began to increase faster and faster.

But the fact is that humans have always been powerful creatures. Our brains, our hands, our ability to co-operate and to communicate, all give us the animal equivalent of super-powers. We are pretty good at creating things: but when it comes to destruction, we are supermen.

If we seek a living animal to remind us of the superpowers of destruction, then perhaps the best choice is a little black bird that looks as if it is wearing a clown's red nose. This is the **takahe**. It is one of those New Zealand specialities.

Back, briefly, to the idea of islands: and the way that island birds often become more energy-efficient by abandoning flight, and taking up the easy life. Before humans arrived, New Zealand had no mammals except, of course, for bats. The islands of New Zealand were unique and strange places: places where the birds ruled. Birds flew or were blown to New Zealand and there – free from the threat of mammals – they evolved, grew and diversified.

Many of them were flightless: the most famous of these were the moas. These were ostrich-like giants. There were 12 species of them, and they ranged from metre-high birds weighing 25 kilos, to three-metre-tall monsters of 250 kilos. They were plant-eaters, all of them: instead of rabbits and deer, New Zealand had giant birds.

TAKAHE

Scientific name: *Porphyrio mantelli*
Size: head and body length around 63 cm (25 in.)
tail length 50 cm (20 in.)
Range: New Zealand
Habitat: grassland, forest
Food: snow grass, other plants

There were several huge and flightless species related to the birds we know: a coot, a duck, a goose. There were also some bizarre New Zealand monsters that were perfectly capable of flight. One was an eagle bigger than any that exists in the world today. It is possible that it was capable of killing the giant moas, swooping down from the air to attack their vulnerable heads and necks.

Humans first came to New Zealand about 1,000 years ago. These were the Maori people. Over the next 900 years or so, they killed and ate their way through the moa population. They killed the giant eagles, too: probably as a matter of self-defence. These giants would have been perfectly capable of dropping down from the sky to attack and kill a grown man. Europeans arrived in the 19th century, and with them came rats and foxes to speed up the pace of destruction.

New Zealand once had a unique collection of living creatures. Practically all of it has gone. It did not need the Europeans to destroy them. The Maori people – despite their less efficient weapons – were just as destructive. They simply took a little longer than people with guns would have done.

The point is not to blame the Maoris of ten centuries back, or the Maoris of today, or European settlers. The point is not to blame anybody at all. The only point worth considering is how to save what is left of the strange birds of New Zealand. The story of the moas reminds us that humans have the power for destruction – and that we have had it for centuries.

But the takahe – along with the kakapo already mentioned, and a group of other strange and unique birds – is still with us. The takahe hangs on in places where the introduced predators, the rats and the stoats and foxes, have been trapped and removed. Takahes have also been introduced to four small islands, where the places they live in can be controlled.

Humans, as the takahe knows, can create and conserve, as well as destroy. The point is not to wail about the past, but to set about securing the future.

29 Queen Alexandra's birdwing butterfly

ELICATE, helpless, beautiful: perhaps butterflies are the best example of the modern relationship of humans and the rest of nature. With a butterfly, we can understand our strength. And we can see the beauty of what we could destroy so easily. We can also understand the wonder of nature from a butterfly. We know that it lives in four stages: first an egg, then a caterpillar, then a chrysalis, which finally hatches out into the winged wonder, the finished adult butterfly. Each butterfly's life is a strange and miraculous story.

If butterflies have a strength, it is in their numbers and their variety. The group of butterflies and moths is a great one for biodiversity. There are more than 100,000 species alive in the world today: doubtless there are plenty more 'unknown to science'. Let us turn at once to the very biggest of them all. This is **Queen Alexandra's birdwing butterfly**.

By butterfly standards they are colossal. The length of head and body is around 7.5 centimetres and the wing span of the female can be as much as 25 centimetres. The males are a little smaller, with a wing span of 18 centimetres.

The butterflies live in a handful of places in Papua New Guinea. They are not animals you see very often, because they spend most of their time in the canopy of the rainforest: that is to say, about 40 metres above the ground, among the leaves and flowers of the highest trees.

Living in a remote place is no protection from the power of humans, as we have seen many times already. Rainforest destruction continues, in Papua New Guinea as it does just about everywhere else in the tropics. The habitat of the Queen Alexandra's birdwing butterfly has been broken up, as areas have been cleared for farming.

Breaking up habitat breaks up populations. There is no

Scientific name: *Ornithoptera alexandrae*

Size: female wing span up to 25 cm (10 in.),
males 18 cm (7 in.)

Range: Papua New Guinea

Habitat: primary and secondary rainforest

Food: larvae feed on vine leaves; adults take nectar

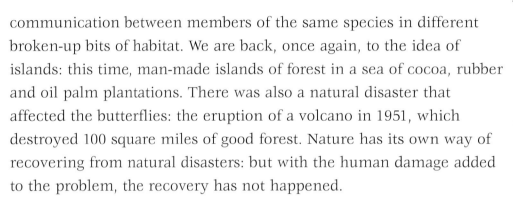

communication between members of the same species in different broken-up bits of habitat. We are back, once again, to the idea of islands: this time, man-made islands of forest in a sea of cocoa, rubber and oil palm plantations. There was also a natural disaster that affected the butterflies: the eruption of a volcano in 1951, which destroyed 100 square miles of good forest. Nature has its own way of recovering from natural disasters: but with the human damage added to the problem, the recovery has not happened.

What is more, the Queen Alexandra's birdwing butterfly is huge and beautiful, and therefore very desirable to butterfly collectors. This is both good news and bad news: the Papua New Guinea government is keen to conserve the butterflies, but the butterflies also fetch a good price in illegal deals.

An area of forest has been set aside for the butterflies, which of course conserves the other species associated with the place. In a rainforest, this always means a lot. There are also projects for rearing butterflies in what are called 'butterfly ranching' operations; again the idea is to allow local people to make money from the local wildlife.

It is a delicate business, and these are, of course, early days. But at this early stage, the Queen Alexandra's birdwing butterfly could possibly become a symbol of the way in which humans can, if we choose, use our power to look after the delicate and fragile beauties of our planet.

30 Mediterranean monk seal

I T'S easy to see how humans can have power over a butterfly: we must now understand that humans also have power over an entire sea. Let's look at the Mediterranean. The Mediterranean has long been considered the most beautiful sea on Earth. In terms of human myths and legends, it is also the most powerful sea of all. Western civilisation, as many of us know it, sprang up round the Mediterranean. Some of our best and oldest stories come from the Mediterranean. It was a sea of adventures, mystery, sudden storms, heroes.

And it was, of course, the eternal provider of food: a beautiful, fish-filled place, a place that was both the highway and the larder of humankind. For humans it was both a permanent challenge and a permanent gift of plenty.

The power of the sea is the stuff of many of these great stories: the helpless human subjected to the power of the sea and the sea-gods. The Mediterranean stood for everything that was wild in nature; and also for everything that was good and kind in nature.

These days, the Mediterranean tells a different story. Not the power of the sea over puny humans: but the power of humans over puny nature. The modern Mediterranean is a tale of over-fishing, pollution, the ever-growing human population and ever-increasing human disturbance.

The animal best able to tell this story is the **Mediterranean monk seal**. These seals were once found on the coast of France and Spain, the Canary islands and in many places in the eastern Mediterranean. Now there are probably fewer than 500 of them left, in three separate populations.

The seals have been hunted for their meat, their skins and their oil. They are a protected species now, but they are still illegally killed by fishermen, who see them as rivals for the fish. And fishing gets harder in the Mediterranean year by year. One of the oldest principles of humans working with nature is this: when in doubt, persecute the predator.

Seals also get caught in fishing nets and drown, because they are mammals like us and need to breathe the air. One of their biggest problems is disturbance, because the Mediterranean monk seals are wary beasts and like to keep to themselves. Disturbance alarms them a lot. A pregnant female who is disturbed by humans will very often lose the pup she is carrying inside her. A female who is feeding a young pup will, if she is disturbed, lose the ability to feed the pup from her own milk. Once again, the pup will die.

The Mediterranean is heaving with people these days. Fishermen, scuba divers, holiday-makers, not to mention the people who live there. This is a sea under huge pressure: and the pressure comes from people. A further problem is pollution. Pollution is a problem in every sea in the world, even the most remote. And the Mediterranean is not the most remote sea; quite the opposite. It is the most accessible: surrounded by people, their waste and their industries, and filled with their shipping. Pollution kills and damages fish that are already in a bad enough state because of over-fishing. This is a problem for fishermen; it is also a problem for fish-eaters like seals. The seal is fast approaching the stage at which it has nothing to eat and nowhere to hide.

At least there are now some conservation measures in place. The Greek government has declared an area of sea as a national park, but fishermen are against it. There is a scheme for rearing orphaned seal pups. There is a reserve on the Turkish coast. There are efforts being made to encourage fishermen to take tourists out for trips to see

MEDITERRANEAN MONK SEAL

Scientific name: *Monachus monachus*

Size: length up to 2.6 m (8.5 ft)
weight up to 300 kg (660 lb)

Range: Mediterranean Sea and Black Sea,
Atlantic coast of north-west Africa

Habitat: sea. Used to breed on open beaches,
probably now prefers deep caves

Food: fish

the seals, for money, of course. The idea is to make a living seal more valuable to fishermen than a dead one.

The Mediterranean still looks beautiful. But underneath the surface, it is quickly becoming one of the world's most beautiful disaster areas. The Mediterranean monk seal can tell the full story. Incidentally, the Mediterranean monk seal has two close relatives: the Hawaiian monk seal, which is also endangered, and for similar reasons – conflict with fishermen, and disturbance. There is another, the Caribbean monk seal. This was hunted relentlessly for its skin and its oil. It is now almost certainly extinct.

31 Californian condor

WE have seen the power of humans over the world's largest butterfly: the fluttering, fragile Queen Alexandra's birdwing. Now let us turn our attention to human power over the most powerful flying creature still living on this planet: the *Californian condor*. I shall not issue the usual warning: that humans could drive this animal into extinction. I do not need to do so, because it has already happened.

But the animal is not *quite* gone. The Californian condor lives, as its name says, in one of the richest parts of one of the richest countries of the world, and it is a huge and spectacular beast. These are very considerable advantages, if a species should happen to need a major conservation programme. Therefore, huge and spectacular efforts have been made to save the Californian condor.

The bird became extinct in the wild when the last remaining wild birds were captured – eight of them. Since then, there have been successful efforts to breed these birds in zoos, and to release their young birds back into the wild. This is a first-rate example of the human determination to beat the Humpty Dumpty Effect. In the case of the Californian condor, conservationists have made truly heroic efforts to put everything back together again.

The Californian condor has a wing span of nearly 3 metres. It is not much smaller than the giant hawk of New Zealand, the extinct monster that probably killed giant moas and possibly killed humans. A full-grown adult Californian condor weighs 11.3 kilos.

Californian condors reached the edge of extinction through a pattern that is growing familiar. People-pressure is the main reason:

big birds need a huge wild area to live in. The condors live almost entirely on animals they find dead. When people moved into the wild, and started farming animals, the condors had no trouble making a living. Dead cows and dead horses were just as good for them as dead buffalo.

But modern farming is a much more closely controlled business and there are very few dead animals left lying about. Also, humans brought guns and they shoot many of the local animals. Often they fail to find the animals they have shot, and leave the fallen beast to the condors. But the condors eat not only the animals they find: they also eat the lead shot that killed them. And the lead, building up inside the condors, slowly poisons them.

Luckily California is proud of its condors, and efforts to save them have begun. Condors have been reared in captivity and released into areas of California that are still wild. So the attempt to put time and fate into reverse begins.

With programmes like this, it is generally a case of six steps forward and five back. Some animals cannot adapt to the wild, other meet with accidents: they hit power lines, they get hit by cars. And even in the remote places, they can eat poisoned carcases and die.

There are now carcases put out for the condors by conservationists. This means the carcases are at least poison-free: on the other hand, eating from a kind of giant bird-table is not quite the same as being a wild bird.

Humpty Dumpty has not really been put back together again: so much is clear. But the programme continues to move forward. There is a plan to have two wild parks, each with a population of 150 birds, and a back-up population of condors in zoos. The extinct Californian condor is still out there and flying, even if it needs a fair amount of human power to do so.

CALIFORNIAN CONDOR
Scientific name: *Gymnogyps californianus*
Size: wing span up to 2.75 m (9 ft)
Range: USA
Habitat: open country
Food: carrion

32 Kerry slug

THERE is another way in which human power can be destructive: and that is more or less completely by accident. The power is used to destroy animals which most humans didn't know were there, animals most people have never even heard of.

In the rainforest, as we know, the destruction of any sizeable area will destroy not only creatures most people have never heard of, but many that *nobody* has ever heard of – animals that are `unknown to science'.

However, my choice for demonstrating the principle of human power-by-accident is a creature called the **Kerry slug**. It is, I know, hard to love a slug: but, as we have seen with the no-eyed big-eyed wolf spider, conservation is not a matter of taste. We cannot only conserve the cuddly animals. We have a duty to all animals: and besides, nature does not work by cuddliness alone.

So let us look at the distinctly non-cuddly Kerry slug. It is quite a pretty slug, by slug standards, which may not be saying very much. Like most slugs, they are large and squashy, and they can alter their shape a good deal: they can stretch out, flatten themselves, or roll themselves up into a ball. They vary in colour and pattern: whitish or yellow spots and blotches on a grey or brown background.

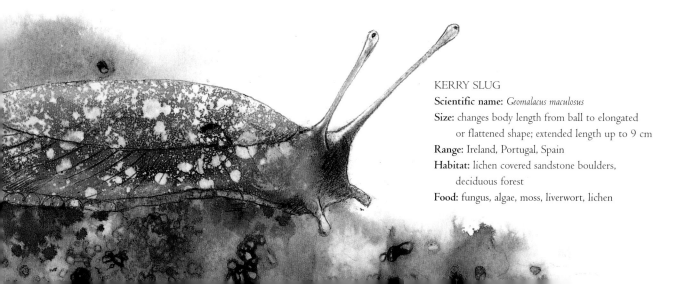

KERRY SLUG
Scientific name: *Geomalacus maculosus*
Size: changes body length from ball to elongated
    or flattened shape; extended length up to 9 cm
Range: Ireland, Portugal, Spain
Habitat: lichen covered sandstone boulders,
    deciduous forest
Food: fungus, algae, moss, liverwort, lichen

They are found, as the name suggests, in south-west Ireland: but also in northern Spain and northern Portugal. The slug is a versatile thing, and can live in two completely different habitats. It lives around boulders that are covered in the strange groups of plants called lichens, or in old forests, around lichen- or moss-covered tree trunks.

It is possible that the slugs' first choice of habitat is woodland; but after their woods were destroyed, they managed to make a new kind of life in the cleared areas. If this is so, they managed to avoid the `tender trap' of specialisation: it is a rare thing for an animal of any kind to survive the destruction of its chosen habitat.

The greatest current danger is to the Portuguese population. Here, large areas of forest are being destroyed, and being replaced by eucalyptus plantations. Eucalyptus trees come from Australia, where they support all kinds of creatures. But in Portugal, they support very little. A tree in the wrong place is a very poor bet for wildlife: and eucalyptus trees are certainly useless for the Kerry slug.

In Ireland the slugs live in a protected area; and there is even talk about captive breeding programmes for them, in order to introduce them to other places in Ireland where they have died out. So far, this species hasn't been greatly studied – slug experts are thin on the ground – and the needs of slugs are not properly understood.

The Kerry slug tells us a very important story. In a way, it is more chilling than the story of the deliberate destruction of the blue whale. Even more destructive than deliberate human power is accidental human clumsiness. Humans are perfectly capable of wiping out a species by a clumsy accident. By a moment's lapse in concentration, we can lose yet another part of life on Earth.

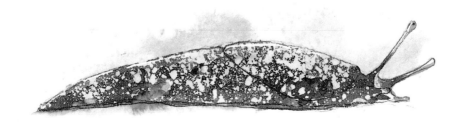

33 Muriqui or Woolly spider monkey

WALK through a maze and eventually you find the centre. And then you try to find the way out again – and it seems that every turning you take somehow brings you back to the centre again. Conservation is like that. No matter which path you take, sooner or later you end up back in the rainforest.

Every figure concerned with rainforests is staggering. It is hard to believe a single one of the basic facts about rainforests. For example, rainforests contain nearly half of all living species of plants and animals – and yet rainforests cover less than two per cent of the surface of the Earth. An acre of forest outside the tropics will contain about four species of tree. An acre of tropical rainforest contains up to 80 species, sometimes even more. An investigation of a single square mile of rainforest in South America revealed 1,100 species of plant. An investigation of a 300-square mile piece of rainforest discovered 500 resident species of bird: four times more than there are in all the forests of eastern North America.

The tiny country of Panama has a little rainforest left within it. There are more different species of plants in Panama than there are in the entire continent of Europe.

The biggest and most important areas of rainforest left are in Brazil. And it is here, in the complex layers and galleries of the forest, that we find the **muriqui**, also known as the **woolly spider monkey.**

MURIQUI or WOOLLY SPIDER MONKEY
Scientific name: *Brachyteles arachnoides*
Size: head and body length up to 63 cm (25 in.)
weight up to 15 kg (33 lb)
Range: Brazil
Habitat: Undisturbed high forest, also lowland and mountain rainforest
Food: leaves, also seeds, fruit, insects

'Spider monkey' is an unexpectedly good name. The monkeys have prehensile tails: that is to say, they can use them for climbing and gripping. They can comfortably hang by their tails alone and, when it comes to climbing, the tail is almost as good as a third arm or leg. When moving at speed through the branches, a woolly spider monkey looks as if it has five legs, all working in a strange and complicated fashion. Its odd way of moving and the impression of more than a fair share of arms and legs gives you the weird idea that you are looking at some kind of nightmare spider, a creature even more alarming than the no-eyed big-eyed wolf spider.

These animals have now reached the point of crisis. There are probably no more than 200-400 individuals left. And we already know the reason for this: habitat destruction. The muriqui can live only in undisturbed forest: the world's most threatened habitat.

The Brazilian forests that lie along the Atlantic coast have suffered more than those elsewhere in Brazil. They have been destroyed to clear land for farming, to sell the timber. In the areas favoured by the muriqui, only two per cent of the original forest is left. This is a disaster.

There are chunks of forest left, some with muriquis in them. But we are back to the business of islands again – the different populations of the monkeys cannot get to each other, cut off by the endless miles of farmland that lie between the islands of forest.

This leads to problems. If a small group of related animals breed together, the flaws and failings of these individuals get worse in their children and worse again in their children's children. This fact is true of humans, and it is true of all other animals. That is why

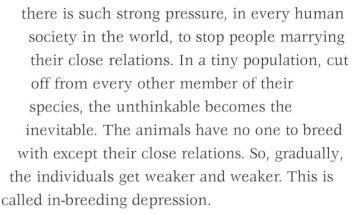

there is such strong pressure, in every human society in the world, to stop people marrying their close relations. In a tiny population, cut off from every other member of their species, the unthinkable becomes the inevitable. The animals have no one to breed with except their close relations. So, gradually, the individuals get weaker and weaker. This is called in-breeding depression.

We are left with a few scattered populations of muriqui, populations too small to avoid in-breeding depression. We have seen, with Californian condors, that some species can be bred in zoos and released back into the wild. But this is not possible with all species. It is extremely difficult to keep muriquis in captivity. This is because very little is known about their diet. It's hard to look after an animal if you don't know what it eats.

The muriqui is in a bad way. The destruction of rainforest has to be stopped: certainly for the sake of this monkey. But rainforests are even more important than we thought. Not just to muriquis: not just to all the uncountable creatures that live in them. They are important to everything that lives on Earth.

34 Golden bamboo lemur

AND so, even as we leave the middle of the maze, we take the turning that leads straight back. Rainforests, once again.

All forests are important, and all forests are disappearing. But no forests matter more than rainforests. And our next creature of the rainforest is a particularly jolly little thing called the **golden bamboo lemur.**

The rainforests of Madagascar are important not just for the golden bamboo lemurs who live in them. They are important for the rockhopper penguins of the Antarctic, and they are important for human beings who live on the opposite side of the world.

We have already talked about global warming when we discussed the rockhopper penguin. Now it is time to look at trees: and the strange fact that trees are important for penguins. And important for the humans who live in cities and never look at a tree.

Global warming happens because of the greenhouse gases that are released into the atmosphere. Over the past hundred years or so, the Earth has been very slowly getting warmer, because humans are putting more greenhouse gases into the atmosphere. These come from industries, transport, the way we heat our homes. And, strange but true, more greenhouse gases are also produced by the cattle we farm for meat and for milk.

What has this to do with trees? More than you would think at first glance, because one of the most important of these greenhouse gases is carbon dioxide. Animals, humans included, breathe in oxygen and breathe out carbon dioxide. Trees do the exact opposite: they take in carbon dioxide: they give out oxygen. So it all works quite beautifully. Or at least, it used to.

The forests of the world play a big part in keeping the world's climate steady. As people destroy the forests, so the climate is forced to change. We are producing more and more greenhouse gases, and at the same time, we are destroying the Earth's system for preventing the build-up of these gases. In short, we have launched a ferocious double-pronged attack on ourselves, and on every other animal on the planet.

So let us turn to our latest rainforest beast, the golden bamboo lemur. Lemurs are primates: that is to say, they come from the same group as monkeys, apes and humans. They live only on the island of Madagascar, which stands off the coast of Africa. Yes: back once again to islands, and the way that islands produce their own special range of animals.

GOLDEN BAMBOO LEMUR
Scientific name: *Hapalemur aureus*
Size: head and body length up to 46 cm (18 in.)
tail length up to 56 cm (22 in.)
weight up to 2.5 kg (5.5 lb)
Range: Madagascar
Habitat: rainforest
Food: bamboo, bamboo creeper, bamboo grass

There are about 20 species of lemur, the smallest the size of a large mouse, the biggest over a metre long. The golden bamboo lemur is medium sized. They are, as the name rightly suggests, bamboo specialists: they eat the leaves and shoots of bamboo. The shoots, oddly enough, are poisonous, and eating them kills most animals. But not the specially adapted bamboo lemur. They are found in a small area of rainforest in the south of the island; they were 'unknown to science' until 1987. Most of the bamboo and forest from which they come has been destroyed, mainly to clear space for farming. The timber trade is also responsible for clearing forests.

There is a proposal to declare an area of forest as a national park. This will have to happen very soon. There are probably between 200 and 400 of the animals left. It has been estimated that the golden bamboo lemur could go extinct as early as the year 2000. Further destruction could set a kind of record: an animal that goes from discovery to extinction in just 13 years.

The lemurs need their forests. So do the rockhopper penguins, whose nesting places have been destroyed by the ever-rising level of the ever-warming sea. So does the rest of the world, if we do not want the planet to continue its disastrous pattern of warming. If the rich world needs the forests that grow in the poor world, it has only one option. To pay for them.

35 Wolf

THERE are, to speak very roughly, three kinds of forest. The forests in the wet places near the Equator are what we know as tropical rainforest. At the very top of the Earth, before you reach the snow and ice of the Arctic Circle, we have the pine forests. And in between, we have temperate forests. These temperate forests are full of green leaves in spring and summer, their leaves turn brown in autumn, and their branches are bare in winter. It is the same pattern in the temperate forests all around the Earth – those that remain.

In some ways, these temperate forests are more important than rainforests. Not only because of what they do – like the rainforests they help to keep the Earth cool – but also because of what they mean to human beings. European people lived for thousands of years on the edge of the temperate forests, for temperate forests at one stage covered most of Europe. There was no escape from them.

Forests were once frightening places. Humans did not feel safe in them. The fear, of forest and of all nature, was one of the reasons why humans were happy to destroy the forests that grew all around them. Then, and even now, many people find wild places deeply frightening.

WOLF

Scientific name: *Canis lupus*
Size: head and body length up to 150 cm (50 in.)
  tail length up to 51 cm (20 in.)
  weight up to 60 kg (132 lb)
Range: northern latitudes
Habitat: wilderness areas
Food: moose caribou, other deer, livestock,

One of the reasons why Europeans found their forests so alarming was because they were the home of the **wolf**. Western children are brought up on stories about wolves, *Little Red Riding Hood*, for example, and they are taught songs about wolves, like *Who's Afraid of the Big Bad Wolf?*

These days, things have changed. It is the wolves who need to go about singing *Who's Afraid of the Big Bad Human?* Wolves have always been considered vermin, like the African wild dog. Since firearms were invented, they have been shot, the shooter believing he was doing the human race a favour. But destruction of habitat, in particular of the temperate forests, is the most important cause of the wolf's decline. Wolves survive in wilderness areas. The animal that was once considered such a threat to humans now only survives as far away from humans as it can possibly get.

Wolves are, despite the horror stories, beautiful and impressive animals. They love the sound of each other's voices. Packs howl for the same reasons that birds sing: to tell other members of their species that they are where they are. The sound of a full pack chorus is one of the most extraordinary sounds in all nature. And perhaps to Western people, brought up to fear wolves more than any other living creature, it is the most frightening.

Wolves, like our domestic dogs, love a social life. They socialise, not with a human owner, but with each other. In their packs, only the top male and the top female breed, just like the African wild dogs. The rest of the pack, all relations, help care for the pups. Wolf society, like human society, is based on sharing and co-operation.

Humans are only now beginning to understand about the wild places and the wild forests, and so we are now only just beginning to believe that the wolf has a place in the world after all. It is just as we begin to lose things that we understand their value. People now go on holiday to look for wolves: once, people would go miles to avoid them.

36 Elk or moose

Let us move on up, then, to the third great belt of forest that encircles the globe. This is the forest of the cold weather, not the rainforest but the snowforest. In some of these forests, there are only a couple of months of the year in which the place is free from frost. Such conditions would kill an oak tree. The trees of the temperate forest, with big broad leaves which they shed in autumn, could not survive in the lands of intense cold, the lands that lie on the edge of the North Pole.

Instead, there are forests of pine, spruce, fir and hemlock. These trees are always green. They have needles instead of leaves, and they carry cones. They are designed for the cold. The shape of each tree is downward sloping, so that the snow will slide off, as it does off a sloping roof.

The further north you go, the fewer species of trees and of animals you find in the forests. The rainforests, as we have seen, have an almost incomprehensible biodiversity. In the tougher conditions of the north, the patterns of life and its variety are much less complicated. That is because it is a lot harder to survive.

The wolf, an endangered animal of the endangered temperate forests, is also at home in the snowforests. We must turn to another animal to represent the forests of the far north.

The animal I have chosen has two names. In Europe it is called the **elk**, in America it is called the **moose**. This is confusing but useful. The coniferous forests go all the way round the world, in an almost unbroken ring, across North America, northern Europe and northern Asia. And, instead of the bewilderingly different varieties of the rainforest, the snowforests give us the same band of species through the same worldwide band of trees.

The elk and the moose are the same species: a giant beast of the deer family, the largest of all deer. Some have colossal antlers and stand up to nearly two metres tall at the shoulder. Size is an important matter in these hard conditions: the further your vital organs are from the surface of your body, the warmer you can stay. The biggest tigers live in Siberia; the biggest bears are polar bears, with brown bears of the coniferous forests not far behind. Naturally, the biggest deer are found in the coldest places.

It will come as no great shock to learn that the greatest threat to animals of the snowforest is the same as the threat to animals of the hot, moist tropical forests – felling the trees. The coniferous forest of the western side of North America has been savaged, with only about 10 per cent of the original forest left.

There is another and more subtle threat, and this is acid rain. Industries release stuff that poisons the Earth. In continents where you get the most industries, you get the most poison. So naturally, you get huge problems in northern Europe and North America. Industries of all kinds release poisons into the air. This is brought down again by rainfall. So instead of pure water, it rains acid. The acid kills the mosses and lichens that grow in the trees, and in a slow, inevitable process over extended periods of time, it kills the trees as well.

No trees means no elk, or moose. So there are attempts underway to stop the falling acid rain from doing any harm. In Sweden the government has been introducing a chemical – lime – which neutralises the acid and makes it harmless. Good idea: but unfortunately the elk eat the lime and it poisons them.

Even without the great biodiversity, even in these far more simple northern forests – once things go wrong, they are too complicated to put right. The cure is as bad, if not worse, than the disease. It is like trying to warm up your cold hands by plunging them into a saucepan of boiling water. The cure will only bring you more problems, and more serious ones. Once again we find ourselves face to face with Humpty Dumpty.

ELK or MOOSE
Scientific name: *Alces alces*
Size: to shoulder, up to 2.8 m (6 ft)
Range: northern latitudes
Habitat: wilderness areas, lakes in summer
Food: leaves, water plants

37 Capercaillie

WE have just travelled north, through three great belts of forest, forests that are damaged and incomplete: from rainforest, through temperate forest to the snowforest. We have seen how all forests play an important role in keeping the Earth healthy, in keeping the Earth a safe place, not just for forest animals but for every species of animal on the planet – including human beings.

Yet humans continue to destroy the forest. Humans, the dominant inhabitants of the great house of the Earth, are smashing up the air-conditioning system. Already, this is beginning to make the house uncomfortable, as global temperatures rise. If we carry on, the air will become less and less fit for us, and for every other animal, to breathe.

So having travelled up from the tropics to the snow-forest, let us make the journey back down again. And as we do so, let us celebrate some of the beasts that survive in the surviving bits of forest. We shall stay for a moment, then, in the dizzy north, and seek another animal that has its place among the conifers and the snows. Let us enjoy the monster bird of the Scottish woodlands: the **capercaillie**. It is about

the size of a turkey: when you first see one it's hard to believe your eyes. There must a mistake, you think. The bird can't be *that* big.

Scotland is a land mostly of bare hills, and it is easy to think that this is the way things always were: rolling, tree-less hills, a bleak and noble landscape. But in fact, the hills were once covered in forest. The trees have been chopped down over the centuries, for fuel, for ship-building, for industry. A few fragments of forest remain here and there: the great north wood. It doesn't take long to see that the hills that still carry trees are the noblest of them all.

Even in the wildest part of Scotland, there is little chance of growing the wood back again, because of the deer. Deer have been allowed to flourish everywhere. They are looked after, cherished. They are fed when the weather gets cruel, as it always does in the long, hard winters. Scotland holds far more deer than would be possible under natural circumstances. The deer have an easy life: and to make things even easier, the animals that once ate them, the wolves, have long been extinct in Scotland. The deer have no enemies.

The deer have been pampered because people will pay a very great deal of money to shoot them. And the deer eat the baby pine trees, if they can get them. A forest will not start to grow itself again if there are large numbers of deer. And capercaillies, and the other creatures of the ancient woods, need forest.

CAPERCAILLIE
Scientific name: *Tetrao urogallus*
Size: length up to 87 cm (34 in.)
    tail up to 28 cm (11 in.)
Range: northern Europe, mountains further south
Habitat: pine forest, some broad-leaved forest
Food: pine needles, shoots

Now, attempts are being made to allow the great north wood to grow itself again. These are successful: the forest starts to spread very rapidly from its edge, given a decent chance. A decent chance means not very many deer.

If you have a scrap of ancient forest, and you want it to spread, the first step is to take the deer away. The second step is to keep them away. You can build big fences that keep the deer out. There is only one problem with that: the fences kill capercaillies. The birds don't see the fences, and fly into them. Big heavy birds, flying at speed: they crash, and kill themselves. In other words, the best way to create perfect capercaillie habitat tends to kill capercaillies. We seem to be having yet another meeting with Humpty Dumpty.

The way forward is to reduce the number of deer all round, so that the forests can grow without fences. Of course, that would make shooting deer more difficult, and deer-shooting is big business. The good news is that these problems don't arise from destroying forests, but from getting forests to grow again. And in a way, these are the most cheering kind of problems to have. In the great Scottish wood, with the monstrous capercaillie lurking in its depths, there is, in the long winter and in the brief, sharp summer, more than a gleam of hope.

38 Iberian lynx

IT seems a while since we last had a cat, and so it is high time to bring in another. We haven't had a cat since the tiger stalked its majestic way across these pages 35 species ago. This is a pity, because cats have always been favourites of mine. Like many of us, I've always had a special soft spot for the family of *felidae*.

And so, as we journey south from the snowforest back into the temperate forests, let us celebrate the **Iberian lynx**, a cat that is small, lovely, and wild – and these days, seems utterly out of place in a part of Europe that prides itself on being modern, up-to-the-minute and prosperous.

The Iberian lynx comes from Spain and Portugal. It is spotty, with powerful paws and wonderful big ears. There are larger species of lynx that live in the snowforests all around the world; in the colder places, as we know, you tend to find larger animals. Further south, in America there is a smaller lynx, generally called the bobcat. But in southern Europe, in the temperate forests, and also in the open, scrub country called the maquis, you find the Iberian lynx.

The Iberian lynx has been having a hard time for many years. Humans tend to take a very simple view of animals that eat other animals. They consider them rivals, and try to get rid of them. Lynxes have long been persecuted, on the grounds that they might kill domestic animals that are worth money: that is to say, sheep and goats. In fact, the Iberian lynx mainly eats rabbits.

The lynx does most of its hunting at night, which is why it needs its wonderful hearing. It has suffered from the destruction of its habitat, the forests and the maquis, as well from fierce persecution by farming people. And carnivores, as we have seen, are always very close to extinction. The bigger and fiercer the animal, the more vulnerable it is.

There are now only about 1,000 Iberian lynxes left, so this is an animal that is getting very close to the edge. The problems are increased, because the animals live in small areas, each cut off from the other. We are back once again to the problem of islands, and of in-breeding depression.

There is only two per cent of Iberian lynx habitat left. The lynxes that remain often get caught in traps set for rabbits and foxes. They are night-hunters, and they are often hit by cars on the road at night. They do, indeed, seem like animals left over from an altogether wilder past.

IBERIAN LYNX
Scientific name: *Lynx pardinus*
Size: head and body length up to 110 cm (43 in.)
    tail length up to 30 cm (12 in.)
    weight (males) up to 12.9 kg (28 lb)
    (females) 9.5 kg (21 lb)
Range: Spain
Habitat: forest, maquis (open scrubby countryside)
Food: rabbits

And that's the trouble, you see. In far too many countries, the undeveloped places and the wild animals that live in them are seen as something slightly old-fashioned. Something rather embarrassing. Almost a sign of failure. A country that still has wild lynxes: can it really be so modern and advanced after all?

Yes, of course, yes. And far more modern and up-to-date than the countries that have got rid of their wild places. As the wild places and the wild beasts that live in them are being destroyed, so more and more are people beginning to appreciate and understand what it is left.

We are really only just beginning to love and respect our wild places – just as we are on the point of destroying them altogether. It's always said that you don't know what you've got till it's gone. Let's hope in the case of the wild places and wild beasts, that it will turn out that we didn't know what we'd got until it was *almost* gone. Many countries have factories and farms. How many have Iberian lynxes? Just two. We must make our politicians rethink their idea of national pride. Wild places should be seen as the pride of the modern world.

39 *Bannerman's turaco*

A FEW pages back, I said how much more cheering it was to talk about the problems of re-growing a forest, than about the problems of trying to stop its destruction. This is all very well so far as it goes. There isn't a lot of point in talking about halting the destruction of the great north wood of Scotland, because practically all of it has already gone. There is just a tiny bit left, and there are good efforts being made to allow these small patches to spread once again, which is all very fine and splendid.

There is a better way of looking after the Earth's forests than chopping them down and trying to grow them back – and that is not to chop them down in the first place. Indeed, it is the only way of avoiding our unwanted companion of these pages, the infernal Humpty Dumpty. It is much more fun to cheer the new dawn of the great north wood – much more cheerful than going on about the destruction of the rainforest. But the fact remains that practically *all* of the Scottish forest was destroyed in past centuries. We still have half of the world's rainforests left.

To think of half the rainforests being destroyed is an absolutely awful business. On the other hand, to think that half is still left – that is still an awful lot. It is still – massively, tremendously, colossally – worth saving. It is one of the most worthwhile jobs on the planet, nothing less.

There is an old saying: where there is life there is hope. The rainforests are filled with life. And this is a book of life. Therefore, it is a book of hope. I can't make it any other way. I have no choice. Nor do any of us.

Back then, to the rainforest, down from the chills of the snowforests and the capercaillie, to the softer weather of the temperate forests and

BANNERMAN'S TURACO
Scientific name: *Tauraco bannermani*
Size: total length up to 45 cm (17.7 in.)
Range: Cameroon
Habitat: rainforest
Food: fruit and berries

the Iberian lynx, and finally into the teeming, impossible rainforests.

Can I possibly tell you what it is like to walk in rainforest? It is like walking underground. You are about 50 metres below where the action is. You walk through a haunting, murky place where you can see nothing but massive tree trunks. There is not a leaf to be seen: they are all far above you. It is up there, in the roof of the forest, in the canopy, that the real life happens.

Down below, you hear the occasional call of a bird, the buzz and chirp of insects, sometimes, the swish of wings as some huge bird flies clear of the canopy. And sometimes you see something: a flash of colour, too bright to belong to a bird, you would think.

But it is a bird. There are some crazily coloured birds up there: and one of the brightest of them all is **Bannerman's turaco**. It is only found in tiny patches of rainforest in Cameroon, in west Africa. The patches of forest are tiny because most of them have been cut down, mainly to make space for farming.

More destruction, more misery. But there is still a fair amount of it left, so let us at once go back to hope again. Around Mount Oku there is an area of 100 square kilometres still standing, still unspoiled. And here, there is a conservation project in place for this bird of ridiculous colours. The project involves the local farmers, as a good conservation scheme must. The idea is to teach the farmers to use the forest without destroying it. To make the forest work for them. To make the forest more valuable standing than it is chopped down.

Miserable people say that a bottle is half-empty. Hopeful people look at the same bottle and say that it is half-full. We look at the rainforests, and say – half-full. But for pity's sake, don't pour out any more.

40 Black coral

WE have made a lightning tour of the world's forests: let us now plunge into the sea and make a tour of the world's oceans. And as we do so, let us examine how important the seas are for the entire planet: every bit as important as the forests. That is because everything is as important as everything else in the great house of the Earth. Everything *depends* on everything else. You cannot damage one thing without damaging everything else as well. It's like asking, which is the most important wall of the house? The answer is, all of them. If you knock down one wall, all the rest are likely to fall down as well. It doesn't really matter which one you destroy: destroy one and you destroy the lot. We need healthy oceans so that the ocean creatures can lead healthy lives: we need healthy oceans so that the creatures of the land can live healthy lives. We humans, being creatures of the land ourselves, have a very good reason for looking after the oceans.

We have just left the rainforest: so let us dive head first into the place that people like to think of as the ocean's own rainforest. By this, I mean the coral reefs. Let us pick on a single, endangered type: **black coral**.

There are about 150 species of black coral, and about 2,500 species of coral altogether. Corals are the most visible animal on Earth: astronauts were able to see the 2,000 kilometre-long coral formation of the Great Barrier Reef of Australia from space.

Coral polyps are small animals, and most species like to live together. They do so in vast numbers. They are small, soft creatures

BLACK CORAL
Scientific name: the family *Antipathidae*
Size: not applicable
Range: all warm seas, some species in cooler temperate seas
Habitat: seas 30-110 m (98-360 ft) deep
Food: tiny animals

that are capable of making for themselves a rock-hard overcoat, as a kind of skeleton. When these small animals come together, they can build walls and towers of coral skeleton. Coral reefs are built of the skeletons of millions of coral polyps.

A visit to a coral reef is as dramatic an experience as the planet can give you. You do not even need breathing apparatus. All you need is a face-mask, perhaps a snorkel. I said that walking in rainforest was like being underground: snorkelling over coral is like flying. Below you, fish that are every bit as bright and weird as Bannerman's turaco lead their lives. Extraordinary colours: dramatic biodiversity: a perfectly unbelievable world.

The main problem affecting black coral is that people like to take chunks of it home as souvenirs of their holiday. Coral makes nice jewellery, jolly ornaments. It is odd that people choose to remember a place where they were happy by helping to destroy it.

Other kinds of coral are destroyed by dynamite, to clear the way for shipping, and sometimes to use as building material. Often these blown-up coral reefs are made into buildings for tourists who have come there to swim and to enjoy the coral reefs. This would be funny if it wasn't sad.

Unfortunately, the sea is particularly vulnerable to the Bottomless Bucket Principle: the belief that there is always plenty more where that came from. And even if this was not the case, another principle would still apply: if I don't take it, somebody else will.

These are principles that are leading us towards disaster. Coral needs more protection, the trade in coral needs proper control, and the seas need areas where the taking of coral is forbidden. As for blowing up reefs – by doing so, you destroy your own natural protection from the sea. It is one more way in which, by destroying nature, we are destroying ourselves and our home.

The sea does not belong to anybody in particular. It belongs to everybody, and to nobody. And that is precisely the reason why the oceans are in such trouble.

41 Codfish

THE next animal to look at is the **cod**, which is sometimes called the **codfish**. It sounds rather silly, I know. Save the cod! We haven't been brought up to think of the cod as a living animal at all. It's a food. Cod is the first fish that British people think of when they wonder what to eat with chips.

Few of us know what a living cod looks like. We think of it as something that comes in a slice, with breadcrumbs on it. Cod has been a favourite food for centuries. The cod is part of our history. The problem is, it may not be part of our future.

If I start to talk about the beauty of the cod, I am not going to be taken very seriously. But it is a rather fine animal, as we can see here: three fins along its back, and handsomely marked. It can grow pretty big as well: up to 12 kilos. There are a fair few meals that can be taken from a big cod. They are highly desirable animals.

That is why they are in trouble. Not in deep trouble: some of the animals we meet here on these pages are down to a few hundred, or even a few dozen. Cod are not in danger of going completely extinct: not yet, anyway.

But there are fewer and fewer of them. Fishing for cod is becoming more and more difficult. Finding the big shoals is no longer straightforward. The problem is overfishing: that is to say, taking too many fish out of the sea. We are back to the Bottomless Bucket Principle; and also, the dreaded thought that if I don't do it, somebody else will. Who owns the sea, after all?

There are constant quarrels between the countries who have fishing fleets, over who has the right to fish where. Britain and Iceland fought out a non-shooting, but highly dangerous, conflict called the Cod Wars in the 1960s and 1970s. The reason for the conflict was simple: there were not enough fish to go round.

People often act selfishly over something that is shared – at least, they will if they can get away with it. This kind of selfishness, the kind that makes everything worse for everybody – including, in the long run, the selfish ones themselves – is called the Tragedy of the Commons. It is all about the inability to share.

The open seas are everybody's property, and everybody's property is nobody's property. No single fisherman, no single fishing company that owns the huge fishing boats that also operate as floating fish-processing factories, and no single country wants to be the one that stands back, and lets the other nations steam in and take advantage of its good sense and decent behaviour.

In other words, everybody wants to stop overfishing, but nobody dares to. Again, it would be funny if it wasn't sad. The Tragedy of the Commons is also a kind of Comedy of the Commons. But it is a gloomy joke.

CODFISH
Scientific name: *Gadus callarias*
Size: weight up to 11.4 kg (25 lb)
Range: Atlantic Ocean
Habitat: ocean bottom
Food: fish

42 Narwhal

Humans have always found food in the sea: they have always found mysteries as well. For humans to go to sea was – and for that matter still is – a move into the unknown.

Let us, as we continue to look at the world's oceans, look at two of the great mysteries of the sea, mysteries which have haunted the human imagination for centuries.

The first mystery is the unicorn, an imaginary animal we have already met in the first chapter, along with the real-life but vanishing scimitar-horned oryx which, it seems likely, inspired the unicorn myth. For years the myth was believed to be the truth. This was because people occasionally found unicorns' horns: not the ringed, antelope horns of the oryx, but the twisting, spiral horns that appear in all the classic pictures of the unicorn.

The horn is no myth, but real. It comes not from prancing horse-like creatures of the imagination but from a member of the whale family, the **narwhal**. The horn is, in fact, an overgrown tooth, and it is mostly the males who carry them. They use them much as deer use their horns: for fierce, ritual combat. Male narwhals have astonishing overhead fencing matches with their unicorn-teeth.

Narwhals live in the northern seas, around the pole, and eat fish and squid. They are in danger because they are hunted. They have, for centuries, been hunted for food. To make them doubly desirable, the horn itself is valuable. It is made, like an elephant's tusk, from ivory.

Narwhals, in their striking weirdness, can stand for all the mysteries of the oceans. We, being land-mammals, think of the Earth as a series of pieces of land, separated by bits of sea. But we have got it precisely upside-down. The Earth is a planet of water, with a few bits of land here and there. The oceans cover 75 per cent of the planet. They also contain an a extraordinary wealth of animal and plant life. The oceans are part of the system on which all life on Earth depends.

NARWHAL

Scientific name: *Monodon monoceros*
Size: head and body length (males) up to 4.7 m (15.4 ft)
(females) 4.15 m (13.7 ft)
Weight: males up to 1,600 kg (3,000 lb)
females up to 1,000 kg (2,200lb)
Range: Arctic seas
Habitat: deep waters, occasionally seen closer to land
Food: fish, crustaceans, squid

The oceans contain almost all the water on Earth: 97 per cent of it. Since water is essential to life, it seems fairly obvious that we should look after the oceans if we intend the planet, and our own species, to have some kind of a future.

The shifting weather patterns of the Earth depend on the oceans and the circling waters. Water that rises from the sea to form clouds eventually falls on the land, not as salty seawater, but as fresh, clean, living water and, because it falls, we are able to water our crops, our animals and ourselves.

We think of the oceans as distant, unknowable places, and so they are: places of mystery, filled with creatures of mystery, many of them still unknown to science. But in another sense, oceans are the most familiar thing to us: we depend on them for our daily bread and for our daily drink.

The people of the land, even those who never in their life see the sea, are as dependent on the oceans as any fisherman. It is one more way in which everything on this planet depends on everything else. The oceans, even those most distant from the haunts of humankind, need to be cherished. For their own sake, and for the sake of every human being on Earth. But, we shall see as we move onto our next animal of mystery and myth, this is not what happens.

43 Dugong

HAVING brought you the unicorn in the last chapter, it is now time to bring you the mermaid. The myth of the beautiful woman with a fish's tail has been part of the human store of strange tales ever since the first sailor went to sea and began to miss his womenfolk back on shore.

The animal that is always supposed to have inspired the myth of the mermaid is the **dugong**. It is hard to think of an animal that looks less like a beautiful woman than a dugong: but the dugong generally gets the credit. Probably this is because of the animal's habit of resting in the water, with the top half of the body exposed. All the same, the sailor who confuses one of these gentle, fat-faced beasts with a beautiful woman must have been at sea an awfully long time.

The dugong is from the family of sea-cows, ocean-living mammals that cannot climb out onto land. They live in the warm waters of the Indian and Pacific oceans, and they feed on the seagrasses that grow in shallow water.

The dugong is vulnerable to just about every bad thing that is happening in the oceans, and there are a fair few of these. For a start, it is hunted for food. Dugongs are large beasts, and the fact that they breed very slowly means that numbers cannot recover quickly from a sustained attack by humans. Hunting dugongs is now illegal in most of the world: but making a law and making people obey it are two very different matters.

The second problem is overfishing. There are so many humans trying to make a living from the sea, and so many fishing nets as a result, that it very hard to avoid them. And dugongs, being mammals like ourselves, breathe the air, and when they get caught in nets, they drown.

The third great problem is water pollution. The coastal waters are always the most polluted parts of the ocean. People tend to get rid of their rubbish – from homes, from farms, from factories – into the nearest bit of water. This flows out to pollute the oceans of the entire Earth: but the nearer the coast, the greater the level of human filth.

Human sewage is the first and most obvious pollutant of coastal water. The second is the variety of poisons running from agriculture into the rivers, and so into the seas. Then there are poisons from industry. All these flow into the sea and poison the plants, the fish, and all other creatures that live there.

The oceans are seen not only as a bottomless bucket, from which we can take anything we need, but also as a bottomless dustbin, into which we can throw anything we don't want. Well, the dustbin is full now, and there won't be a dustbin van coming to empty it.

Meanwhile, the dugong continues, where it can, its calm and lovely existence. It may not be as beautiful as a mermaid, but, perpetually snacking in the vast warm bath of the Earth, the shallow tropical seas, it lives a rather beautiful life. Where it is allowed to, anyway.

DUGONG
Scientific name: *Dugong dugon*
Size: length up to 3 m (10 ft)
    weight up to 400 kg (880 lb)
Range: Indian Ocean and Western Pacific Ocean
Habitat: shallow tropical and sub-tropical coastal
    and inland waters
Food: seagrasses

44 Kemp's ridley sea turtle

THERE is something almost pathetically trusting about the turtles that live in the sea. All land-animals have distant relations that once lived in the sea. The sea is not only essential to all life on Earth: it is the place from which all life on Earth came in the first place.

Some animals stayed in the sea, of course. And some land-animals later returned to the sea. And, superbly though they cope with everything the seas throw at them, they still have the unmistakable mark of land-animals.

They cannot breathe underwater, like fish, but instead, come to the surface and breathe the air as humans do. Whales, dolphins, seals, penguins: wonderful swimmers and divers, but all of them must breathe the air. So do turtles.

Whales and dolphins give birth to their young out at sea. Seals must come onto land. Penguins come onto land to lay their eggs. And so do turtles. Returning to land is hard. As we humans know, walking on land is very different to swimming.

It is hard for a human to swim 'like a fish', as the saying goes. Our bodies are not really made for swimming. Even the fastest of human swimmers is nothing compared to a seal: he is simply making the best of a bad job. If we wear flippers on our feet, we can swim much better. But try walking in flippers: at once we become slow, clumsy and likely to flop over on our faces.

It is the same thing for seals, penguins and turtles. They are much better at swimming than we are: not nearly so good at walking. But they must come ashore to breed, and walk as best they can. When a big female turtles hauls herself onto a beach to lay her eggs,

KEMP'S RIDLEY SEA TURTLE
Scientific name: *Lepidochelys kempii*
Size: shell up to 89 cm (35 in.)
weight up to 41 kg (90 lb)
Range: Atlantic basin, nests on Gulf of Mexico
Habitat: waters of the Gulf of Mexico
Food: preferred food is crabs; also fish, jellyfish, other crustaceans, molluscs

she has taken on a desperately hard job. She cannot run away from any enemy, she can only flop her way up her beach, flop down and lay her eggs, and then, with a good deal of luck, flop back.

A flopping turtle is a sitting duck: the easiest animal in the world to kill. And many have been caught for meat. The eggs they lay get taken by humans. If most of the females who come ashore to lay eggs are killed, and most of the eggs they lay are eaten, then the animal is going to go extinct very swiftly.

That has been happening with many species, and the female population of Kemp's ridley sea turtle is down to less than 1,000. To add to their troubles, many of them get caught in fishing nets and drown.

However, there is some good news for the Kemp's ridley sea turtle. The 20-mile beach on which they have always laid their eggs is now protected by the Mexican government. A second colony has been established in Texas. There are now rules that shrimp fishermen must fit their nets with devices that stop turtles getting caught.

This is cheering stuff. Because a female turtle coming ashore to lay her eggs is so vulnerable, it seems unfair to take advantage of her helplessness. Kemp's ridley sea turtle, helpless, reliant entirely on the goodwill of a busy and often hungry human population, can stand not just for itself and for the oceans, but for the whole planet. That makes it doubly pleasing to report some good news on the subject. Humans can, if they choose, help the helpless. The numbers of Kemp's ridley sea turtles are slowly rising.

45 Flightless cormorant

ANGER: OIL ON BEACH. Practically everybody who has been
to the seaside has seen such a sign. And practically all of us
have trodden in a patch of oil at the seaside, or worse, sat on one.
Filthy, stinking, sticky, disgusting: it takes an age to wash it off your
skin. And it's almost impossible to wash it out of your clothes.

Imagine if you had feathers. For a bird, oily feathers are not just
messy. For a bird, oil is death.

Oil comes into the sea from boats. Most of this oil is waste from
the engines. If you don't need the oil any more, you can simply throw
it into the sea. Back to the principle of the Bottomless Dustbin. Ships
are not allowed to do this: but cleaning your engines out in harbour
takes time, and time is money, especially in shipping.

There is a more dramatic way in which oil finds itself in the sea,
and that is when a large tanker, carrying oil as a cargo, has an accident.
We have already heard about the disaster of the Exxon Valdez.

I saw an oil disaster in Wales, when a tanker called Sea Empress
ran aground and spilled its huge cargo of
oil. I shall never forget the stink of that
day, nor the way the sea moved in sticky
gloops, like treacle. Nor the sight of a
duck, swimming hard with just its head
and neck above the surface. It was going
down with all hands.

I have chosen a bird to stand for the
dangers of oil pollution, an animal which
is, like the Kemp's ridley sea turtle,
uniquely vulnerable, uniquely helpless.
This is the **flightless cormorant**.

FLIGHTLESS CORMORANT
Scientific name: *Phalacrocorax harrisi*
Size: head and body length up to 100 cm (39 in.)
weight up to 4 kg (8.8 lb)
Range: Galapagos Islands

As we know, birds that live on islands often develop flightlessness, like the kakapo, the flightless parrot of New Zealand. The Galapagos islands of the Pacific are home for the flightless cormorant.

The bird's flightless style of living, swimming everywhere, makes them especially vulnerable to oil spills. And a small population, as we know, means that a single disaster could wipe out an entire species. Small, random spills from oil-dumping ships have put the flightless cormorant in trouble, A big oil slick, from a super-tanker disaster like Exxon Valdez or Sea Empress, would send the birds extinct overnight.

The population is now about 1,000 birds, which gives them no margin for safety. They never travel more than a kilometre from their home shores, which means that a small oil slick in the right place would kill them all. They are another example of nature in its full helplessness. They evolved flightlessness as a sensible, useful way of leading a more energy-efficient life. Humans, in their constant search for oil, are the most energy-inefficient creature ever to walk the planet. The cormorant evolved flightlessness, and there is no going back. Humans must learn to become energy-efficient for their own survival. At the moment, we are heading in precisely the opposite direction.

46 Bittern

LET us leave the oceans for a while, but stay with water. Turn to the places where land and water are found together: the damp, soggy places of the world called wetlands.

Sometimes you find wetlands on the coast, where the land and sea meet and make some kind of compromise. Here the water is neither fresh, nor as salty as the sea: and here, in these brackish waters, you find animals and plants that specialise in these difficult conditions.

In other wetlands, the water is fresh, fed by rivers and rainfall rather than the ocean. Fresh water is always teeming with life. Humans often love these wild, wet places: perhaps it is because we, too, need fresh water. We appreciate the beauty of these places because the need for fresh water is something we share with our fellow land-animals. Lush, wet places are for that reason deeply satisfying.

But they are also in deep danger. Humans need more and more water. Or, at least, they take it: to water crops, for industries, for the daily lives of our towns and our cities. The way we use water is wasteful and damaging. All over the world, wetlands are threatened by draining. Wetlands are drained for farming, and they are drained because humans want the water.

Once you take away the water, you destroy everything that makes a wetland special. A wetland that is no longer wet has become something else entirely. If it's left to itself after the water has gone, the water plants die, land plants take over, and the wet-loving animals can no longer make a living. If the land is turned into farms, or places for houses, then very few wild animals can live there at all.

This continues to happen all over the world. So the first animal I choose to represent wetlands is a bird from a country where almost all the wetlands have been destroyed. This is Britain, and the bird is the **bittern**.

The bird was once common, because there was once an awful lot of wetland. In particular, bitterns were common in an area of East Anglia called the Fens: 300 square miles of damp, soggy land. The main plants there were reeds, which grow like a giant field of corn, and which grow only in wet places. In the last couple of hundred years, the Fens have been drained. There are only three square miles of fen left. There is a project which is trying to make another square mile, but it is fighting Humpty Dumpty at every step.

Bitterns are not globally endangered, but they are almost extinct in

Britain. The places you can find them are all owned by conservation organisations who maintain, and even recreate, the wild, wet reedbeds that the bitterns love.

Bitterns wade through the reeds, hunting fish, eels, birds and mammals. They are very hard indeed to see: skulking, secretive things. But in the spring, the male birds, though they stay in hiding, tell the world that they are there. They call out for female company: they boom. This strange noise, like a small cow, or perhaps the biggest frog the world has ever seen, is one of the spookiest sounds there is, especially if you hear it at dawn, when the mist is rolling over the marshes. It's strange to think it was once a common sound in Britain.

But now, most of the wet places in Britain have gone. Indeed, it is remarkable and wonderful that there are any bitterns left in the country at all. Wonderful that wet places are being made again. We cheered the attempt to build a new snowforest in Scotland, and we can cheer the new square mile of fen, too. There are still untouched wetlands. But as with untouched rainforests, we must seek to stop them from being destroyed.

BITTERN
Scientific name: *Botaurus stellaris*
Size: length up to 80 cm (31.5 in.)
      wing span up to 135 cm (53 in.)
Range: Europe, northern Asia
Habitat: lowland swamps
Food: fish, amphibians, insects

47 Chinese alligator

As we travel on through this book, the pattern remains the same. When humans and animals want the same thing, the animals feel the pressure. Fresh water is one of the most valuable things on the planet, so it's hardly surprising that humans and other animals have been fighting for it. The more humans there are fighting for water, the more they win.

Back, then, to the country with more people than any other on Earth: to China, and to represent the wetlands of this vast and crowded place, what better than the **Chinese alligator**?

We have discussed the way that big and fierce animals are always especially vulnerable, the way that sharp teeth are no help in the fight against extinction. The Chinese alligator is sharp-toothed enough, but no whopper compared to some members of the family. The biggest it gets is no more than about two metres. We like to think of these toothy reptiles as incredibly fierce, living entirely on humans, but the Chinese alligators are not nearly big enough for that. In fact, they eat mainly snails and mussels, with some fish, insects and small mammals.

These alligators were once fairly widespread, but now you find them only in the Yangtze valley: which brings us back to islands and the vulnerability of small populations. There are about 500 Chinese alligators left in the wild. They like shallow beaches and cane thickets, and they're at home among the wetland plants. What has damaged them most has been the taming of these wetlands, the draining of land for farming, the felling of the cane thickets. As this happens, the population breaks up into small groups which cannot reach each other: another problem we have met before.

Humans are capable of changing everything about a place. They can take a wild river, and the pools, lakes and swamps all around it – all that is known by the name of wetlands – and turn the river into a shipping canal, a watering can for crops, a dump for rubbish and various poisons. They can turn wetlands into farming land, or into places for people to live. And it's only when all this has been done that they have the afterthought: what about the wildlife?

This has been the pattern, from the ancient developments of Europe and the more recent developments in North America. The same pattern is followed by the rest of the rapidly developing world. It is the aim of conservation to turn that afterthought into a forethought.

The Chinese government is now establishing conservation areas for the Chinese alligator. There are continuing studies of the species, which will establish more clearly what the Chinese alligator needs to survive in the wild. The main need is obvious enough. It needs wetlands: it needs its places that are wild and wet.

CHINESE ALLIGATOR
Scientific name: *Alligator sinensis*
Size: up to 2 m (6.5 ft)
Range: China
Habitat: river, lakes, ponds
Food: snails, mussels, fish, insects, small mammals

48 Goliath frog

IT doesn't take much to destroy a wetland. It only takes a very small amount of meddling to change a wetland for ever. People who live in the developed parts of the world hardly ever see a big river that has not been tamed. The banks are often built up with stone and concrete, so that the river always runs in the same place. It is made to run straight and true, instead of winding about. Its border of trees and reeds is cut down. The places where it floods are barricaded off. Its bottom is dredged, so that instead of running now an inch and terribly fast, now many feet deep and almost still, it runs at an even depth, an even speed.

Wild rivers are not like this. I have made many visits to the Luangwa valley in Zambia, where the wild Luangwa river changes its route every year. One year a stretch of water may be the main course of the river, but the next, it could be nothing more than a pond.

When humans change the way the waters move, they change an awful lot of other things too. The animal I have chosen to stand for the dangers of this kind of change is the largest frog in the world, and for that reason it has the excellent name of **Goliath frog.**

The Goliath frog really is a massive beast. It can weigh up to 3.6 kilos and, with its legs stretched out, it can reach 76 centimetres. Each eye can be as much as 2.5 centimetres across. It is a giant.

It comes from the rapids and waterfalls of the rivers that flow through a small strip of forest in Cameroon, in Africa. Goliath frogs neatly combine the problems of rainforest and of wetland. They also live in a very small area, which also gives them all the problems of island populations.

These frogs spends almost all their time in the water,

once they are fully adult. At night they search along the edge of their rivers for food: insects, shellfish, even smaller frogs of different species.

To add to its problems, the Goliath frog is a local delicacy itself. It's hardly surprising: the frog, being huge, has a huge amount of meat. What is more, anything that is huge and outlandish is going to attract human interest. There are always people from the developed world who want to have such animals as pets. Very big specimens of this animal have been known to change hands for US$2,000.

But the main reason for the frog's vulnerability is water. While they are growing up into adult frogs the tadpoles need certain plants to feed on. These plants are extremely particular about where they grow. They can only thrive in very clean water, with a lot of oxygen in it, and only a slight natural acid content. Change these precise things, and the plants can't live, which means the tadpoles can't survive, which means the frogs will go extinct. And being a small population, once they start to go, they will go very quickly indeed.

If the forest is cut down, if the water courses of the river are changed, then everything about the habitat will be different. And the Goliath frog will be no more.

GOLIATH FROG

Scientific name: *Conraua goliath*
Size: length (legs extended) up to 76 cm (30 in.)
    weight up to 3.6 kg (8 lb)
Range: Cameroon, Equatorial Guinea
Habitat: rapids and waterfalls in dense forest
Food: insects, crustaceans, molluscs, amphibians

49 Puna grebe or Junín grebe

I F ever there was an creature to show the perfect fragility of the wetlands, it is the **puna grebe**, sometimes called the **Junín grebe**. It is also, for that matter, the perfect example of an island species, even though it lives in the mountains of Peru.

The puna grebe lives only in Lake Junín, a large shallow lake 4,000 metres up in the mountains. All the grebe family are great swimmers and divers, not much given to flying. The puna grebe, living in this single lake cut off from the rest of the world, has gone the traditional way of island birds: it has become flightless. The lake used to hold several thousands of them: busy, sociable birds, normally found in flocks of a dozen or so. The females lay eggs: the young birds ride on the backs of the males, while the females dive to get food for them.

The numbers of puna grebes have fallen very quickly. Fifty years ago, there were still thousands of them. Twenty-five years later, they were down to just one thousand. Another ten years and there were less than 400. Now there are 20 or so. Extinction looks very close to a certainty. But there is no giving up on them: not while there are puna grebes left to save.

Island populations are, as we know, vulnerable to a single disaster, and a single disaster is exactly what the puna grebe has suffered.

Mining goes on in the mountains all around Lake Junín. This has two effects on the lake. The first is that poisons are washed into the lake as a matter of routine. These poison the fish. The animals that eat the fish get, in a single meal, all the poisons the fish has taken on in a lifetime. And grebes eat poisoned fish for every meal. They take in more and more poison, meal after meal, and in very high doses.

PUNA (or JUNÍN) GREBE
Scientific name: *Podiceps taczanowskii*
Size: length up to 38 cm (15 in.)
Range: Peru
Habitat: Lake Junín
Food: fish, insects

To make matters worse, the lake is also used to generate electricity for the mines. Water is required suddenly and in large amounts: when this happens, the water level of the lake drops dramatically, by more than a metre. Fish are stranded and killed, nests of puna grebes are cut off from the water. The puna grebe is a flightless bird but a beautifully designed swimming machine, wonderfully suited to its specialised environment – until, that is, humans once again shift the goalposts.

There have been conservation efforts made for this dwindling species. On one occasion, four of them were shifted to a lake that does not have the pollution problem of Lake Junín. Unfortunately, this lake had a fishing problem. The four puna grebes all disappeared: it is believed they got caught in fishing nets and drowned.

The search continues for another site, where another population of puna grebes can be established by moving a few more of them from Lake Junín. Meanwhile, further efforts continue, to persuade the Peruvian government and the mining companies that they should work together with conservation organisations to save Lake Junín and, by doing so, save the puna grebe.

50 Snow leopard

WE have reached the half way stage of this book and, to celebrate, I have chosen another cat. We leave the wetlands as we do so, and continue our grand tour by soaring up into the mountains. There are two ways of making this grand tour. We could look at all the different kinds of wild habitats. Or we could look only at the habitats that are in danger. But as it happens, we don't have to worry which one we choose – because either way we'd end up with exactly the same tour.

The fact of the matter is that every kind of wild habitat in the world is under some kind of threat. This isn't to say that the situation is hopeless, and it certainly isn't to suggest giving up. But everywhere you find wild places, wild habitat, wild animals, you also find people, and the pressures of people's needs. Everywhere you look in the world, there are problems: in the forests, in the wetlands, at the bottom of the ocean, at the top of the highest mountains. But I'm not telling you about them in order to make you feel miserable and depressed.

There are problems. All right. So let's solve them. It's as simple – and as difficult – as that. I don't mean to make you miserable by saying that this animal and that animal is in danger. No: I want the animal itself – by its beauty, by its charm, by its ugliness, by its fierceness, by its gentleness, by its weirdness – to inspire you to join the fight to save it.

How can anybody think of the **snow leopard** and not wish to go out and save it – and the mountains where it lives? I would

SNOW LEOPARD
Scientific name: *Uncia uncia*
Size: head and body length up to 130 cm (51 in.)
tail up to 100 cm (39 in.)
weight up to 75 kg (165 lb)
Range: mountains of central Asia
Habitat: mountain
Food: mammals

like to say that the snow leopard is the most beautiful and the most extraordinary of all the cats – but then all the cats are wonderful.

We know that the bigger and fiercer the animal, the more vulnerable it is. That puts the snow leopard in a difficult situation to begin with.

Snow leopards live in the mountains of the Himalaya, hunting mostly in places too high for trees to grow. They live in some of the most difficult country in the world: places where few humans ever go. This has not stopped humans from affecting them.

Snow leopards live in environments that are very difficult for animals: and therefore the animals they can kill are thin on the ground. They're all pretty rare and hard to find. For that reason, a snow leopard needs a huge area of mountain to hunt in. If you're looking for an animal to stand for the vast open spaces of the world, the snow leopard is a good choice. Few animals on Earth need quite as much space.

They live in places that are always cold, and often frozen and covered in snow. Their coats are much thicker than those of cats that live in the warmth of the lowlands. They have so much fur on their paws that it makes a kind of snow-shoe. Despite the difficulties of travelling in the mountains, people

have made the journey there to kill snow leopards for their fur. No animal that lives in small numbers and over huge spaces can take very much hunting. It is now illegal to sell snow leopard pelts, but it still goes on.

The snow leopards' problems do not stop there. The animals they prey on are themselves hunted by humans, for their meat. That means the snow leopards go short of food, and starve. They also eat small animals, rodents like marmot and pika, but these are often poisoned by farmers, who see them as pests. That poisons the snow leopards.

A snow leopard that cannot catch wild food will often turn to domestic animals. That creates a classic people/wildlife problem. It does seem terribly unfair. First humans kill the snow leopard's natural prey. Because they have no choice the leopards turn to the animals humans keep, and they are punished for it. Unfair: but this whole book is about unfairness.

There are snow leopards to be found in over a hundred reserves, which is very good news indeed. It is not quite as good as it sounds, because snow leopards need so much land. Reserves are never big enough for a wide-ranging species like this, and there are always going to be clashes with people. Compensating people for domestic animals that have been killed is another way of making it easier for humans to co-exist with the snow leopard, one of the loveliest animals on Earth today.

But let us move on to the second 50 animals in this bestiary by repeating the guiding principle of this book. Where there is life, there is hope. The snow leopard is another animal that can stand for hope.

51 Volcano rabbit

IT doesn't matter. A little bit of damage here and there: it really doesn't matter. It doesn't affect anybody else, it's just a small thing. Hardly an earth-shattering matter, is it, to destroy just this little bit here to make life easy this week, or this year?'

This is the principle that humans have always worked on. And as more and more humans now live on the Earth, doing more and more little bits of damage here and there, we are beginning to see that it does matter.

A lot of humans each doing a small amount of damage adds up to a disaster of colossal proportions. That is one of the main subjects of this book. And a small bit of damage in one place affects people in other places. It affects neighbours, it affects people you will never see in your life. And ultimately, it affects the entire world: a small piece of damage to the Earth is like a small piece of damage to a house. A small hole in the roof lets in the water and rots the wood that holds up the ceiling. Soon, the whole thing is rotten and the ceiling falls in.

Small amounts of damage on mountaintops create havoc lower down the slopes. We can see this happening in the destruction of mountain forests. They are being destroyed all round the world, for the usual reasons: to use the wood for fuel and for building, and to use the land that is uncovered for farming.

Trees in a forest hold the soil in place, and the soil in turns holds the water that falls as rain. Forests release water gradually. Many of the great river systems of the world start in the mountains. Half of the world population depends on the water that flows in rivers from the mountains of the Himalayas.

But as the mountain forest is cleared, so the whole system changes. The exposed soil does not hold the water any more. Instead, the water, with nothing to stop it, washes the soil away, leaving the place bare and impossible to farm. The uncontrolled flow of water creates mud-slides and floods many miles away. These are not only bad for wildlife: they kill people and destroy their homes and the ways they make a living. Damage in the highlands leads to disaster in the lowlands. To damage a small thing is to damage everything: that is the way the Earth works.

And to stand for this principle of damage to the mountains, let us turn to a jolly little animal called the **volcano rabbit**. It is the smallest member of the rabbit family and it lives only on four volcanoes in Mexico, in the pine forests at heights of up to 4',250' metres. They shelter in clumps of grass called zacaton.

Volcano rabbits also suffer from the island problem: small populations and the threat of the single disaster. The single disaster is happening in slow motion: the pine forests are being cleared, and the zacaton grasses are being eaten by domestic animals which farmers put out to graze on the slopes. The grass is gathered to make thatched roofs and also burned to make it grow again, providing fresh growth for the domestic animals. But the fires kill the volcano rabbits.

VOLCANO RABBIT
Scientific name: *Romerolagus diazi*
Size: total body length up to 32 cm (12.6 in.)
Range: Mexico
Habitat: pine forest on volcano slopes
Food: vegetation

There are conservation plans for the volcano rabbit, which involve working with the people of the region. There are also programmes to re-grow pine forest and zacaton grasses. This is good news for rabbits. It also good news for humans.

52 Yak

MOUNTAINS are among the hardest places in the world to make a living. It is very cold in the high mountains, and very few plants can grow there. That makes it difficult for the plant-eating animals, and almost impossible for those who eat the plant-eating animals. The snow leopard knows this better than most.

Those of us who live in the lowlands cannot help but admire any animal that can make a living in the very high places. In the Himalayas you find two species who have managed very well indeed: the **yak**, and also the human. Humans have survived because of the amazing ability of the yak to live in this, one of the toughest places on Earth.

Yaks are shaggy cows of the mountains and a hundred years ago they were found in large herds, a common sight in the high mountains of Tibet, China and India. You could regularly see gatherings of several thousand. They climb to astonishing heights, and actually make a living at 5,000 metres. They look clumsy and unbalanced, but that is completely misleading: they are wonderfully talented climbers.

They are also superbly adapted for the cold, with their big bodies and their thick coverings of fur. So much so that, when the summer comes, the yaks go *up* the mountains, away from the bright summer growth and back towards the perpetual snows of the heights.

The humans of the mountains have lived with domestic yaks for centuries. They use them as beasts of burden, they eat their meat, they make clothes from their fur and they use their milk to make butter, which they put in tea. The domestic yak is a tough, serviceable domestic animal for the mountain people, but a poor thing beside a real wild yak. For a start, it is only half the size. A wild yak can weigh up to a ton.

And that is where the trouble comes from. The wild yaks have also been slaughtered for their meat, and there are only a few hundred of them left. This is not only bad news for yaks: it is bad news for mountain people. They need the wild yaks. It is the custom to allow wild yaks occasionally to mate with the domestic yaks.

YAK
Scientific name: *Bos mutus*
Size: head and body length up to 3.25 m (10.7 ft)
    tail length 2 m (6.6 ft)
    weight (males) up to 1,000 kg (2,205 lb),
    (females) 330 kg (728 lb)
Range: high Himalayas
Habitat: mountain
Food: vegetation

This puts a regular addition of strength and vigour into the breed. It would be bad news for the mountain people if their domestic animals went soft on them.

There are about 12 million domestic yaks. These eat a good deal of the mountain vegetation, leaving little for the wild animals. They also spread diseases into the wild population which, as it gets smaller, is less able to withstand such setbacks.

Wild yaks continue to be shot, even though this is now illegal. The trouble is that it is extremely difficult to enforce the laws in the wild places where yaks live. There are plans to establish reserves for the wild yak. The story of the over-hunting of the wild yaks is one more example of the Bottomless Bucket Principle. At least people are beginning to realise the hopeless futility of such a principle. And they are beginning, just beginning, to do something about it. There are still wild mountain places for the yaks to live in, that is the best of the news. All the yaks really need now is to be left alone.

53 Pink fairy armadillo

THE desert must be the strangest landscape of all. Most of us are used to things being in the way when we look: buildings, trees, cars. It is very strange, then, to find yourself looking out at nothing. And a kind of nothing that seems to go on for ever.

Mostly, we think of desert as rolling sand-dunes and baking heat: and a fair bit of desert is exactly like that. But a desert is just a place short of water: and there are cold deserts as well as hot ones. And there are rocky deserts and there are also strange gravel plains, which seem like an endless tray of cat-litter.

Deserts really do seem to be the places that life forgot. Places that are no good to man or beast. And although it might seem that the sooner we clever humans do something to stop them being deserts, the better it would be for everything on the planet, that isn't the case at all. Life is an amazing business, and this book, my bestiary, is a collection of things that amaze me. There is only one thing more amazing than the desert; and that is the fact that animals find a way of living in it.

I have flown in a microlight above the Kalahari desert in Africa and watched fish eagles. These water-loving birds were hunting frogs. Frogs? In the desert? But there were thousands of them. It had just rained, the heaviest rains for more than thirty years, and there were plenty of frogs. For years, frogs had been lying beneath the ground, waiting for this moment. When the land dried up after the last good rain, they dug themselves in, and wrapped themselves in a transparent envelope of skin. They looked as if they were wrapped in cling-film. There they stayed, in a state of rest far deeper than sleep, until the rain came to free them. These frogs can remain that way for years. But the rain comes at last, and they emerge briefly to splash and swim and eat and breed, and leave young that will in turn bury themselves beneath the desert and wrap themselves up in cling-film.

All desert animals must be specialists. A life with very little water is a hard and difficult one. And so for the first desert animal, I have chosen a member of one of the weirdest groups of animals on Earth: the **pink fairy armadillo**.

Armadillos are armour-plated mammals that are very good at digging. The largest, the giant armadillo, can be well over a metre long; the pink fairy armadillo is the smallest, at 12-15 centimetres. It is a mammal, like us, and naturally mammals occupy us humans more than any other group. This book lives up to the traditional human bias in favour of ourselves. I have chosen more mammals than any other group. Mammals are the best studied of all animals: we know a very great deal about lions and tigers and apes. But no one knows much about the pink fairy armadillo.

PINK FAIRY ARMADILLO
Scientific name: *Chlamyphorus truncatus*
Size: head and body length up to 15 cm (6 in.)
weight up to 92 g (3.25 oz)
Range: Argentina
Habitat: desert
Food: mainly insects

It is found in the central and western areas of Argentina, in South America. No one knows how it lives, how the animals relate to each other, or how they breed.

Practically all that is known about them is that they are declining. As humans take up more and more space on the planet, so they change the face of the desert. They have turned vast areas of desert into farmland: hard and poor farmland, to be sure, but humans are ever resourceful.

By doing this, they change the nature of the desert. Once again, the goalposts of evolution have been moved. The desert animals can no longer live their traditional lives. There is increasing concern about the pink fairy armadillo: an animal rarely seen because it spends so much of its time underground. How can we set about protecting an animal if we don't even know how it breeds? Meanwhile the desert changes all around them. It is a hard way of life they have chosen, but it is the only one they know. If the land changes, they cannot change with it.

54 Addax

W E cannot help but admire the animals that make a living in the desert. Humans learn to live in difficult places on Earth by having bright ideas, and then telling other humans about the ideas. That is true for every difficult place on Earth, from the desert to New York City.

Other animals tend to work the slow way. An antelope is not going to invent a heat-proof tent for desert living, or a way of growing its own favourite plants. Non-human animals cope, in the main, by changing their very nature: by changing their bodies.

This is something that happens not overnight but over long periods of history. When we find an animal that is perfectly adapted for life in a hard and difficult place, it looks just a little bit like the work of a genius. In a way it is: but it's not a sudden breakthrough, a discovery, a moment of a crazy inventor crying: 'Eureka!' It's the work of many, many centuries.

That, in a way, is even more impressive than human ingenuity. To consider the **addax** is to marvel. An addax is, if you like, its own work of genius. For it is the master of the desert.

ADDAX
Scientific name: *Addax nasomaculatus*
Size: length up to 1.7 m (5.5 ft)
height to shoulder up to 95 cm (3 ft)
weight up to 130 kg (287 lb)
Range: Chad, Mali, Mauritania, Niger
Habitat: desert
Food: vegetation

The addax can live without drinking: a huge advantage in a place where there is no water. It needs only the moisture it gets from the plants it eats. Plants? In a desert? Certainly: small, and few, but the plants are there. Some plant-eating animals live in a land of plenty: you need only stretch out a paw, or lower a head, and you have breakfast before you.

It's quite different in the desert. Traditional human desert-dwellers are nomads: they roam from place to place, looking for the best pasture, moving on before they have destroyed it, coming back when it has grown again. The addax works on the same principle: forever roaming. It has a long stride, and its wide, splayed hooves spread its weight out over the ground. That means it can walk with great efficiency over the loose sand – and everyone who has walked along a beach knows how tiring it is to walk in sand. The addax is built to endure: to roam for ever.

What it's *not* built for is speed. That makes it an easy target for human hunters. These days, there is an additional problem: it suffers from humans who want nothing more than a good look at an addax. In a way, I don't blame them: I would love a good look at an addax myself. But chasing addax is a disaster. Tourist vehicles chase the

addax but the animals can't afford the energy they spend in these
long periods of high-speed escape. Speed is not what they are good at.
They are built to endure: and pursuit from vehicles takes away their
ability to endure. An exhausted addax is simply not going to be able
to make one of its endless night marches to new scraps of desert
pasture. So it will die of starvation, or plain exhaustion.

But this isn't the principal problem that faces the addax. The fact
is that the desert itself is changing: changing beneath their elegant
and efficient splayed hooves. Drought is the biggest worry of all.

Drought? I have just been telling you how good the addax are at
coping with dry conditions. But humans dig deep for water that lies
beneath the desert: they pump it out and use it to water crops on
the desert's edge. As they do so, the desert itself becomes drier.
Meanwhile, the areas that are watered become too wet for desert
plants.

It is a strange thought: that the animal most superbly adapted for
coping with dry conditions is in danger from dryness. It is, if you like,
a perfect example of the mess we humans are making of things.
Humans seek to improve the desert, and in doing so they spoil it.
And they spoil it not just for the addax: they spoil it for themselves.

55 Grevy's zebra

THE desert is changing. The ancient areas of desert are being made drier: and in the meantime, humans are creating new areas of desert, which is even worse. This is bad news for desert animals: and it's very bad news indeed for humans.

The **Grevy's zebra** is not an animal of a deep desert, like the addax, or the scimitar-horned oryx that we met right at the start of this book. The Grevy's has learned how to live in dry places: but not the very dry places. Semi-arid country: that is what the Grevy's likes.

Some people say that the Grevy's is the most beautiful of all zebras. Its stripes are narrower and finer than those of the commoner kinds of zebra, and there is a certain elegance about it. I've chosen the Grevy's because it is probably the most endangered of the zebras. The dangers come from humans, as we have grown to expect.

GREVY'S ZEBRA
Scientific name: *Equus grevyi*
Size: length up to 3 m (10 ft)
  height to shoulder up to 1.5 m (5 ft)
  weight up to 430 kg (960 lb)
Range: Ethiopia, Kenya, Angola, Namibia
Habitat: semi-arid scrub and grassland, semi-desert
Food: grass

Humans have always longed to get topsides of the desert. To make the desert alive with crops and livestock: this is a dream almost as old as humanity. What humans have succeeded in doing is making more and more deserts: and these are far worse than the deserts they came across in the first place.

Human tend to start their farming on the edge of the desert. That means taking away the plants that grow there naturally. Sudden rainstorms come: and when rain falls in the desert, it is a dramatic event. When it rains, it comes down in torrents. And that washes away the soil, because there are no longer plants growing to keep it there. Once the soil has gone, nothing will grow. Nothing at all: not crops, not even natural desert plants. What humans have done is to take a desert where it was very hard for anything to live and to turn it into a place where it is absolutely impossible for anything to live, humans included. This is called desertification, and it is laying waste to great areas of the planet. In hard figures, new desert is being created at the rate of 20 million hectares, or 49 million acres, a year.

The pumping of water onto the desert, to make it teem with crops, seems the most wonderful idea: a boon to humanity and to the world. Surely, it seems, humans are actually improving the planet: making the world a better place. But it does not work that way. The water runs out, and the desert becomes, as we have seen, even drier. When the water dries out, it leaves minerals and salts in the soil. And nothing at all can grow there.

Oil exploration has made countries rich, but has also led to vast areas of desert being chewed up: and desert life cannot take much interference.

The Grevy's zebra is losing out. Irrigation schemes have stolen the water from areas of semi-arid grassland, leaving them wholly arid and completely lifeless. Meanwhile, in areas of decent grasses, the zebras face ever more intense competition from domestic cattle and goats.

Desert animals are always hard to count. There cannot, ever, be very many of them, because there is not much food and they need to roam over very large areas. But it is estimated that numbers fell by about 70 per cent in the 11 years up to 1988.

There are now a number of reserves for Grevy's zebra, but there is never enough room. Zebras need the freedom to roam from one reserve to another: a wildlife corridor. Disturbance by tourists has been a problem, but tourists do bring money with them. Money from tourism makes it more desirable to save the animals the tourists seek. In its beauty, the Grevy's zebra has a fighting chance.

56 Desert tortoise

THERE seems to be no limit to the human talent for destruction. We have looked long and hard at the rainforest, which is the richest place for life on Earth. Here, the rich pickings of timber are among the many things that encourage humans to destroy them.

Humans can destroy the rich places: and they can destroy the poor ones. A desert is a tough enough place to live: but humans have a knack of making it worse.

Deserts are very tough places: they are also extraordinarily delicate. If you drive over a patch of desert plants just once, you are likely to destroy them for a century. There is not much soil for a desert plant to grow in: if you take away the small bit that exists, you have spoiled all possibilities of life.

Desert life has always existed on the very edge of the possible. That is its beauty, its strength, its fascination, and its fragility. It takes a very great deal to live in the desert: it takes very little to make life in the desert impossible.

And so, for the last desert animal, let us turn to the **desert tortoise**. The desert tortoise is familiar with just about every problem that desert animals face. Desert tortoises live in the southern US and in Mexico; in the Mojave and the Sonoran deserts. They were once pretty widespread, but now live in small pockets, which brings to them all the usual dangers of island species.

DESERT TORTOISE
Scientific name: *Gopherus agassizii*
Size: length up to 38 cm (15 in.)
Range: US, Mexico
Habitat: dry scrub, mountain slope
Food: plants

A single disaster could wipe them out: but in the meantime, they are beset by problems, especially in the US.

For a start, many are taken from the desert for the pet trade. They are also taken for food in some places. Many are killed by vehicles: a tortoise responds to danger by withdrawing into its shell. That is an effective defence against a dog, but it doesn't work with ten-ton lorries.

There are increasing numbers of farm animals grazing in the desert scrub. These trample on the tortoises and kill them. Ravens follow the livestock onto the desert, because they can find food around cattle. But they also turn on the young tortoises and eat them.

The desert tortoise's habitat has changed, because people in the US are now building homes in the American deserts. That brings road construction and more agriculture. Add to that mineral exploration, harvesting of wild vegetation, and dumping of poisonous waste – and you have a habitat in deep trouble. These developments would bring trouble to the most robust place on Earth: and a desert is the most delicate of all places.

The rich and developed countries do a very great deal of complaining about poor countries with rich wildlife recourses. We watch television programmes about the tigers of India, the black rhinoceroses of Africa, and wonder at the terrible mess that these poor countries are making of things. In the meantime, the rich countries carry on destroying the few remaining wild creatures of their own.

57 Przewalski's horse

GRASS is not just a plant. It's a world. Grassland is one of the Earth's great habitats, and therefore, like all the great habitats, it is endangered.

Grass is not just the stuff you get in a lawn. There are 10,000 different species of grass. In Africa you can walk for miles in country where the grass grows higher than your head. Some species of grass in other parts of the world grow even higher: up to 30 metres.

Grass is food for many animals. The big grazing – that is to say, grass-eating – mammals dominate the grasslands so far as the human eye is concerned, but hidden among the grass-stems are vast numbers of insects that in turn become food for insect-eating birds and mammals. Grasslands teem with life.

PRZEWALSKI'S HORSE
Scientific name: *Equus przewalski*
Size: length up to 2.45 m (8 ft)
height to shoulder up to 1.4 m (4.75 ft)
weight up to 340 kg (750 lb)
Range: China
Habitat: open grassland and semi-desert
Food: Grass

The thing about grass is that it grows from the bottom – not, like most plants, from the tip. That means you can bite the top off, and it just carries on growing. If you do that to a young tree shoot, you kill the tree before it has got going. But grasses survive and prosper even while being eaten: it is one of the most ingenious tricks of all life on Earth.

Grass can even survive burning: and in grasslands, fires are often started by lightning. Grasslands are found in areas of low rainfall. There is not enough water in the system for huge numbers of trees.

And the grazing animals contribute to the success of the grasses by eating the trees before they get going. The animals help to keep their own habitat in perfect order for themselves – and for the grasses.

Grassland is found all over the world, in hot and in cold places. You are most likely to find grassland in the middle of huge continents, where the rainfall is naturally low. The African savannahs are the most famous areas of grassland, and we shall turn to them in a moment. First let us look at the grasslands of the central Asian steppes, and at **Przewalski's horse**.

This is the only wild horse left. The last authentic report of a sighting was in 1964, but there are claims from observers that herds still found in central Asia are true Przewalski's horses, and not domestic horses gone wild.

Domestic horses are found all over the world, and they still have a good deal in common with their wild ancestors. They are built for speed, so they can run away from their enemies, and they are tremendously sensitive, in their senses of sight and hearing and smell, so they are always aware if there are predators around.

Like all grazing animals, Przewalski's horse must eat large amounts of grass every day: foraging with its head down, its ears cocked and its

eyes watching. That is how the grazers of the great open grasslands work.

The great trouble with grasslands is that they are so desirable. They are so good for growing grasses. Therefore people turn to them to graze their own domestic grass-eaters: cattle, cows, goats and, for that matter, horses. They also use them to grow their own preferred kinds of grass: that is to say, corn.

The great American prairies, once the home of 60 million buffalo, are now the great corn-growing areas of the western world. The central Asian steppes have also been tamed, with ever-greater intensity, for thousands of years. Przewalski's horse has suffered in the competition with domestic animals for grass and especially for water.

Like many grass-eaters, Przewalski's horse takes fairly well to life in captivity. There is a strong zoo-based population, and there are programmes underway to restore the animals to the remains of their wild habitat. The animal itself needs to be protected but, more than anything else, the small amount of wild grassland that is left in its original range in central Asia needs to be kept safe for the wild grass-eaters. Wild grassland is precious stuff. That is true for central Asia, and true for the rest of the world.

58 Giant anteater

GRASSLANDS are not home just to grass-eaters. There are the great carnivores, the meat-eaters that feed on the giant grass-eaters. And there are other animals, that make a living in less obvious ways. Perhaps the oddest of all of these is the **giant anteater** of South America.

It is a strange-looking beast, all right, with a more or less cylindrical snout. It is at the same time a specialist and an all-rounder. It specialises in the eating of ants and termites: but it can eat them anywhere that colonies of these insects can be found. It just happens that grassland, under the stresses of modern times, is one of its more successful homes.

Giant anteaters were once found all over South America, in rainforest as well as grassland: in the very wet places, and the very dry places.

Give them an adequate supply of ants and termites and they will find a way of making a living: and they managed to do so in practically every possible habitat in South America.

But these days, giant anteaters are declining at a very great rate: and they are only really holding their own in the grasslands. An anteater is quite brilliant at finding ants and termites with its sensitive nose, and equally brilliant at eating them with its long sticky tongue that can measure up to 60 centimetres.

It is also quite brilliant at digging them out with its long, powerful claws. And the claws make it quite good at self-defence: a puma or a jaguar would think twice about taking on a well-armed giant anteater.

But what it's not quite so brilliant at is escaping from people. As ever, the problem is people. People have killed giant anteaters for all kinds of reasons. Some are killed for food. They are killed because the claws and tails are prized as trophies – that is to say, they are killed for fun. They are also killed because it is believed they attack cows

GIANT ANTEATER
Scientific name: *Myrmecophaga tridactyla*
Size: head and body length up to 130 cm (50 in.)
tail up to 90 cm (35 in.)
weight up to 39 kg (86 lb)
Range: Central and South America
Habitat: all habitats from rainforest to open grassland
Food: termites, ants

and people, which is nonsense. Anteaters are only dangerous to ants.

There is also the problem of fire. We have seen that grasses, which grow from the bottom, can survive fires. Therefore, if you set fire to grassland, you kill the tree-shoots that are competing for space and, more important, you prompt the grass into a bout of fresh green growth. That is exactly what domestic cattle want most.

Grasslands are always going to have natural fires. But humans regularly set grasslands on fire on purpose. They do this so that there will be sweet new grass for their cattle. That doesn't worry most wild animals, who can fly or run or dig their way out of trouble. But fire kills giant anteaters in large numbers. They are slow, and their long fur burns fast. Whenever there is a big burn, giant anteaters get caught.

There are giant anteaters to be found in protected areas, which brings in the usual problems of island populations. What is needed is more protected areas – and better protection for those areas.

59 Cheetah

GRASS grows. It does so, like all plants, by taking its energy, more or less directly, from the sun. Every living thing needs energy. And the point about animals is that they are not plants: that is to say, they cannot get their energy straight from the sun. So they eat the plants, and get their energy that way. Therefore, the grasslands, which have untold numbers of grass stems, are home for many animals that eat grass: the grazers.

Grass is difficult to eat. It's very tough stuff. That is why humans can't eat it: they don't have the equipment to deal with such a tough plant. The equipment required is a set of very strong chewing teeth, and a powerful stomach.

These specialist grass-eaters live in the big open spaces of grassland, often gathering together in large numbers. It is much safer to be one of a crowd than to be out on your own: the more ears and eyes around you, the less likely you are to be taken by surprise. That is why our own tame grass-eaters still like to live together in herds. Our sheep and cows are in no danger from fierce animals: but they feel happier as part of a crowd. It is their nature.

Like every other wild habitat, grassland is dangerous. There are many grazing animals in a grassland habitat: and just a few meat-eaters. These are animals that get their energy, not from the sun, not from plants, but from plant-eaters.

The thing about grassland, when the grass is short, is that you can see for miles. It is very hard to creep up on an animal in the open grasses. You need to be sneaky, and lay an ambush. Or you need to be clever, and to work as a team. Meat-eaters use exactly these methods. But one animal, the great specialist hunter of the open grasses, uses the simplest tactic of all. Pure speed.

This is the **cheetah**, the fastest runner on the planet. It's a cat, but it's the only cat that cannot retract its claws. Its claws are forever open on the ground, like spiked running shoes. How fast is the cheetah? In short, explosive bursts of speed, a cheetah can reach 120 kph. A cheetah in full flow is one of the grandest sights on the planet. It runs so fast that its hind feet actually land ahead of the front ones at each huge galloping stride. Small antelopes are its favourite food, because cheetahs are small and light, as big cats go.

Cheetahs were once found all over Africa and a good deal of Asia. There were probably 28,000 of them in the 1950s; only half that many in the 1970s. But the human greed or need for grasslands has taken

CHEETAH
Scientific name: *Acinonyx jubatus*
Size: head and body length up to 1.5 m (5 ft)
tail length up to 81 cm (32 in.)
weight up to 66 kg (145 lb)
Range: Africa, western Asia
Food: antelopes, warthogs, hares, ground birds

away their homes and their prey, and the cheetahs have gone with them. They are now found only in Africa, where there are between 5,000 and 12,000 animals, with another small population of 200 or so in Iran.

Cheetahs do not breed easily in zoos, and so there is no fallback, no captive population. We must look after the remaining grasslands of the world for them – or we lose them. The future, the only future, is in the vast national parks of Africa. That is not a bad future, as futures go. But one of the mottoes of conservation is that nothing is safe. Everything must be watched.

60 Marine otter

WE have one more stop to make on our tour of the world's endangered habitats: or to put it another way, our tour of the world. There is, as we have seen, danger everywhere: danger in the high mountains, danger in the forests; danger in the oceans, danger in the deserts, danger in the grasslands. We end the tour by looking at some of the animals that live in the great cross-over area of the world's habitats, the place where land and sea come together. We turn to the coast.

The coast is a special place for many of us humans. It is the seaside, the place for holidays. These narrow places between dry land and the open ocean come sometimes in dramatic cliffs, where the land falls several hundred feet in a sheer drop to the sea, and sometimes in long beaches, where the land slopes gently into the water. The coast is varied and the sea is always shifting, moving in and out of the land with the tides. It is not quite the open ocean, not quite firm dry land. It is a habitat, or rather a series of habitats, all of its own.

The sea-waters of the coasts are rich. They hold much more food than the deep oceans. That means they hold more life. That is the good news for the wildlife of the coasts. The bad news is that the coast is, obviously, near the land. That is to say, near to humans.

We shall start our tour of the coast by looking at one of the most delightful of all mammals: the **marine otter**.

There is no more charming sight in nature than a marine otter swimming on its back.

Its main food is shellfish, for which it can dive deep. Marine otters live all along the Pacific coast of South America, and there are probably about 1,000 of them left. They suffer from the classic problem of coastal animals: people.

The otters were once killed for their fur, and that is the reason their numbers fell. There are now several reasons why they cannot build up their numbers again. Reason one is because the killing of otters continues. An otter skin is extremely valuable. It has been estimated that an otter skin is worth as much as a fisherman earns in three months. It is inevitable that some otters will be killed for their skin, even though this is against the law.

Marine otters are also killed because of the vermin problem. Humans are violently against any animal that competes with them. Fishermen believe that otters take the fish they need to make a living, and so they kill the otters. Otters also get caught in fishing nets, and, being mammals, they drown.

The marine otter is one of those mammals we know little about: after all, it is hard to track small, swift and mobile animals about the sea. Their needs and their way of life are not properly understood. It's difficult to work out how to save an animal if we don't know what it needs to live.

Clearly, the first step is to cut down on the illegal trade in otter fur, and to try and ease the conflict between fishermen and otters. People need to feel proud of the otters they share their coast with, and to believe that otters are more valuable alive than they are dead.

In short, we want the local people to change their entire attitude to wildlife. It sounds impossible but, all over the world, people's attitude to wildlife has changed dramatically in the last 20 or 30 years. These changes have already brought about triumphant moves in conservation.

There is no reason why wiser attitudes to wildlife, wiser attitudes to the planet, should not spread still wider. After all, we are all in trouble if they don't.

MARINE OTTER
Scientific name: *Lutra felina*
Size: head and body length up to 76 cm (31 in.)
tail length up to 36 cm (14 in.)
weight up to 14 kg (31 lb)
Range: Argentina, Chile, Peru
Habitat: Pacific coast
Food: crustaceans, molluscs, fish

61 Queen conch

SEEING living beasts in the wild is one of the greatest joys a human can experience. But again and again people seek beautiful animals – and want them dead. That is the case with the **queen conch**.

Shellfish have always attracted people, because they are lovely, and because the hard part, the shell, can be kept. People love to collect things. It's not enough to see them: they must be owned as well.

This is fine if you collect shells on the beach: but collecting living animals and killing them for the beauty of their shells is a sad business. And it is leading the queen conch towards extinction. The queen conch likes coastal waters around the Caribbean. This brings a lot of people-pressure: the waters of the Caribbean are home to a great world-wide holiday industry. And wherever the shallow waters of the coast are near human populations – which is most places – the queen conch is declining sharply.

The queen conch is caught for food just as much as for the beauty of its shell. The conches that live in deeper water used to be fairly safe, but now scuba divers can get to them easily. Any animal that lives in a coastal region is likely to be subject to the usual problems of overfishing: back once again to the tragedy of the commons.

The good news is that in the few areas of the Caribbean that are remote from fishing pressures, there is a still a good population of queen conches. But these are scattered and vulnerable, another example of the problems island species face.

The conch requires a decent, sensible management programme, and a ban on scuba-diving for conches. Conservationists are researching the possibilities of farming the conches and building an industry based on the captive breeding of conches. If this is effective, it would leave the wild population undisturbed, and able to build itself up again. If that is the answer, it lies a good way in the future. The important thing now is to control conch-fishing. And control – that is to say, working to prevent the tragedy of the commons – is one of the hardest problems in all of conservation.

QUEEN CONCH
Scientific name: *Strombus gigas*
Size: length up to 20 cm (8 in.)
weight up to 2.5 kg (5.5 lb)
Range: Caribbean Sea
Habitat: sea bottom near islands and coral reefs
Food: algae

62 Shark Bay mouse

THERE are different kinds of coast all over the world. There are soft, muddy estuaries where the rivers meet the sea, places rich in food and therefore rich in wildlife. There are the mangrove swamps of the tropics, the salt-marshes of colder places. There are the cliffs, the beaches, the dunes. Coast comes in many different forms, much of it endangered. The meeting of the land and the sea is an important place for wildlife; and an important place for humans, too.

Holidays, homes, hotels, heavy use of beaches: none of these leave room for wildlife. Miles from people, beaches are soiled by human rubbish: thrown from ships, washed from land, ending up piled together on beaches. The worst of this rubbish is oil, as we have seen.

Coasts are especially vulnerable and delicate places, and the next coastal animal I have chosen is an especially vulnerable-looking creatures. This is the **Shark Bay mouse**, also called the shaggy mouse, or shaggy-haired mouse. It used to live on the mainland of Western Australia, in a place called the Peron peninsula, but it now seems likely that it lives only on Bernier Island.

Shark Bay mice live on sand dunes. Until very recently, dunes were thought of as wasteland. But in fact, sand dunes are special places, with special species of plants that can cope with the tough, almost impossible conditions of sandy soil and sea salt.

In many places, sand dunes are being properly appreciated for the first time. In some of them there are programmes to get the dune plants to grow again. You can see areas of popular seaside walks fenced off. Here, the plants can grow again and the life of the dunes can be re-established.

These programmes, often small enough, signal a big change that has taken place in the world's attitude. A place once regarded as a waste of space is now seen as valuable; important; beautiful; worth saving. It is a small step and every small step is worth cheering.

Back to the Shark Bay mouse. It has lost practically all of the area in which it used to live. The good news is that the mouse responds happily to breeding in captivity. The population on Bernier Island seems safe, though it needs constant watching. Introduced predators like domestic cats could cause immense damage in a very short time.

The main problem is protecting the remaining dune habitat. There is talk of building populations of Shark Bay mice back in mainland areas where the duneland remains, or can be restored. The Shark Bay mouse is vulnerable: but it is a tough little survivor too, given the right conditions. It is our job now to make sure that the right conditions are what it gets.

SHARK BAY MOUSE
Scientific name: *Pseudomys praeconis*
Size: total length up to 23 cm (9 in.)
weight up to 50 g (1.75 oz)
Range: Australia
Habitat: sand dunes
Food: plants

63 Coelacanth

P EOPLE often call the **coelacanth** a 'living fossil'. This isn't a particularly helpful name, but if ever a living animal looked like a fossil, the coelacanth does. It looks as if it's already stone: carved from rock, impossibly moving through the sea without sinking.

The coelacanth comes from a group of fish that once lived in great numbers in a period from 80 to 370 million years ago. The coelacanth is the only one of that group left, and it created a scientific sensation when one was discovered in 1938. Brought on deck by a trawler, it was more than one and a half metres long and weighed over 60 kilos. Everyone thought the entire group had gone extinct 60 million years ago.

This is a good story about the persistence of life: an encouraging one, too, in that animals seem to resist extinction. The coelacanth seemed to have an ability to tough it out. Or at least, an ability to get lucky.

The coelacanth is a weird-looking fish, and it lives an appropriately weird life. It spends the days hiding in underwater caves, rather as a bat roosts in caves until nightfall. Then at night the coelacanth goes out to hunt for smaller fish along the coasts of the Comoro Islands in the Indian Ocean.

The reason they had gone undiscovered for so long is simple: there aren't very many of them. They are just about hanging on. An expedition using a submarine worked out that there was a world population of just over 200. Coelacanths are surviving, but not exactly thriving.

Its rarity, its oddness, the vivid tale of the living fossil, has made the coelacanth a must-have item for museums and collections. That made the fish extremely valuable. We had the absurd situation of science killing off an animal before our eyes, because of the extremely interesting fact that it was still living. There were 11 specimens caught in 1986, for example: a population of 200-odd cannot stand losses at that kind of rate.

Scientists have become more responsible towards coelacanths lately, and trade in the animals is now illegal. Instead, there is research to see what the coelacanth needs, if it is to continue to survive as a living fossil. The worst news is that an *illegal* trade in coelacanths has started up: there are still people who believe that various bits from a dead coelacanth make you live longer.

The coelacanth is, as I say, a good story. The story caught the imagination of over-eager collectors: but it has also caught the imagination of the world. The world is reluctant to let things go, once its attention has been attracted.

In this book, I have enjoyed telling good stories like this one, and talking about animals that have caught the world's attention: animals like the cheetah and the tiger, the black rhinoceros and the blue whale. But not every animal has the good fortune to attract the world's attention: and I have relished in bringing you the obscure and the unheard-of, along with the attention catchers: animals like the Kerry slug, the Shark Bay mouse, the no-eyed big-eyed wolf spider. All these animals have stories too, and good stories.

Now, on the coast of the Comoro Islands, we will end our tour of the world's habitats. We have seen that every type of habitat is in danger. We shall now make a tour of the animal kingdom. And I'm afraid we shall find exactly the same thing: that every type of animal is in danger.

The coelacanth was able to tough it out, or get lucky. So let us continue hoping. And more: let us continue working. Both these things, hope and work, are essential. On that note, let the tour of the animal kingdom begin.

COELACANTH
Scientific name: *Latimeria chalumnae*
Size: length up to 1.9 m (6.5 ft)
weight up to 9.8 kg (22 lb)
Range: Comoro Islands, Mozambique, South Africa
Habitat: undersea caves and steep slopes
Food: fish

64 Chimpanzee

ATOUR of the animal kingdom traditionally starts at the bottom and works its way up to the top. We're not going to make our tour this way. That's because the truth of the matter is that there is no top, and no bottom.

People have always talked about the higher animals and the lower animals – as if some animals were better than others. As if the best of all were the great apes, because they are most like us. As if anything that is like us humans has got to be pretty amazingly wonderful.

The idea is basically silly. People talk about the history of life, and talk of the age of reptiles, the age of mammals, the age of Man. But all along, it has really been the age of insects. After all, there were far more insects in the world than there were dinosaurs, and than there are humans now. What is more, there are far more different kinds of insects. And for much longer – ever since life on Earth began – it has been the age of bacteria, the first and smallest and simplest specks of life, that have existed for as long as life, and will continue to exist as long as life carries on. It always has been, and always will be, the age of bacteria.

A fish is not a failure because it is not a frog. A frog is not a failed lizard. A lizard is not a failed bird. A bird is not a failed mammal. A 'lower mammal' is not a failed ape. An ape is not a failed human.

Life on Earth is not about animals getting better and better and better. The dinosaurs were not failures: they dominated the Earth in all the ways that large animals could, for 100 million years. They did not die out because they were no good: it took an enormous accident to kill them. Mammals did not succeed because they were better than dinosaurs: they could not begin their dominance until the great accident gave them their chance. The dinosaurs' reign of 100 million years is something to make humans feel humble. Humans have been around for less than ten million years.

This is why I am not starting with beetles and working up. I am starting with the **chimpanzee** and then considering many other equally valid forms of life. Including beetles, yes, and fish and eagles and toads as well. Life is not a tower with humans on the top: it is a mosaic. A mosaic is one single picture made up of hundreds of thousands of tiny parts. If any tiny part is taken away, the picture is not as good as it was before.

On then, to the chimpanzee: the closest relative to the human. How close? Amazingly close. Remember the willow warbler and the chiffchaff? Two birds that look so much alike, it is almost impossible to tell them apart. You can only do that with certainty if they sing: a willow warbler warbles down the scale, while a chiffchaff sings 'chiffchaff'.

Every animal, including us, carries in its body the building blocks of life with which the animals of the future are made when the animal comes to breed. The difference between the building blocks of the willow warbler and the chiffchaff is *bigger* than the difference between the building blocks of the humans and the chimpanzees. To be precise, the difference is 1.6 per cent. In other words, there is 98.4 per cent of us humans that is just the same as a chimpanzee. So let's face it: humans are part of the wild animal world, and the wild world is part of us. We are animals: just like toads and fish and willow warblers and chimpanzees. We should be proud.

Being closely related to humans does not make life safe for chimpanzees. Quite the reverse. It is reckoned that there were once several million chimpanzees living in Africa: now there are about 300,000. They live in wet tropical forest: rainforest.

CHIMPANZEE
Scientific name: *Pan troglodytes*
Size: (males) height up to 1.8 m (6 ft)
(males) weight up to 70 kg (154 lb)
Range: equatorial Africa
Habitat: various, rainforest to open savannah
Food: fruit, insects, plants, meat

We have discussed the rainforest often enough already in this book, so I don't need to go over the dangers again.

Chimpanzees face further dangers. Humans want chimpanzees, because of their closeness to humans. They want them for research, as pets, as entertainers in circuses. For every chimpanzee that makes it safely from Africa to captivity, another ten die on the journey. Most of those that make it are brought out of their wild places for wasteful and downright silly reasons. For chimpanzees, the closeness to humans is not a blessing but a curse.

There are conservation laws in place to protect chimpanzees, but these are not properly enforced. There is too much money in the chimpanzee trade. The countries where the chimpanzees live often have troubles of their own, with wars and other kinds of unrest and disturbance.

The outlook for chimpanzees is not good. If we treat our nearest relatives like this – what hope is there for the rest of life on Earth?

65 Javan gibbon

As we race through the animal kingdom, visiting as many different groups as possible, you may ask why I have chosen these particular animals. It's a fair question. There are many endangered animals in the world, many many many. So, as we make this lightning swoop, why these animals and not others?

I have chosen them partly because, like every other animal in this book, they are endangered. And I have chosen them because they represent different groups of the animal kingdom. But also – I had better admit this now – I have chosen them because I like them.

Well, why not? I have my favourites in everything. I like music, I like books, I like people: but I have my favourite music, my favourite books, my favourite people. So here are some of my favourite animals. I have talked already about biophilia: well, I am full of biophilia, and so is every sensible person. Here are some of the animals that make me want to stand up and cheer.

The last animal we met, the chimpanzee, is wonderful: a tool-using, brain-using near-relation. I have chosen one more primate – that is to say, one more animal of the ape and monkey kind – and that is the **Javan gibbon**. I've never seen one, to tell you the truth, but all gibbons are wonderful. To be in the rainforest and to hear the dawn greeted by the various families of gibbons is not something you can easily forget.

Gibbons whoop. They whoop in chorus every morning, just as the birds sing at dawn, and for the same reason. They whoop to tell every other gibbon: this bit of rainforest is ours. And across the valley, the reply comes rolling back in another torrent of whoops: fair enough, but remember, *this* bit of rainforest is *ours*.

The second wonderful thing about the gibbon, after its wild singing, is its acrobatic performance. These long-armed, tail-less monkeys work their way through the forest swinging from branch to branch by their arms. The forest is full of wonderful acrobats of every kind, but the gibbons – perhaps because they are so close to humans, yet so much more acrobatic than us – seem to be the most spectacular of all.

JAVAN GIBBON
Scientific name: *Hylobates moloch*
Size: head and body length up to 84 cm (33 in.)
     weight up to 9 kg (20 lb)
Range: Java
Habitat: forest
Food: fruit, leaves, small invertebrates

I have said that the Javan gibbons are rainforest animals, so I need hardly go on about the kind of danger they are in. The rainforests of Java have been destroyed: about 98 per cent of the gibbons' original habitat has been cleared for agriculture. There is a small piece of forest left in which more than 1,000 Javan gibbons still live. There is also a captive breeding programme which, in time, hopes to introduce Javan gibbons back to the areas of forest from which they have been wiped out by people who kill gibbons for food, or sell them for the pet trade. If the last two per cent of forest can be saved, then the Javan gibbon has a shred of hope.

66 Humpback whale

ALL whales stir the imagination. I have only seen whales once, and it was one of the great biophilia experiences. Their size; the ruthless hunting that has plagued them ever since humans learned to throw a spear; the extraordinary efficiency of whale-hunters ever since the harpoon-cannon was invented: all these things stir great admiration and pity.

But the **humpback whale** is extraordinary and exciting even by whale standards. I have said that gibbons are wonderful, because they sing, and because they are acrobats. Well, the humpback whales are just the same.

Whales and dolphins have large and complicated brains: only the brains of humans are more complicated. These sea-living mammals are – must be – extremely intelligent. But they are not intelligent in a human way. They have an intelligence we can hardly begin to understand.

They are great communicators, these whales, and the humpback is especially gifted. Humpbacks sing long and complicated songs: recordings bring these songs to us, to listen to in our living rooms. It's hard to listen to them: they're so wild, so spooky, so remote from our understanding. It is the most thrilling and disturbing thought: the humpbacks are intelligent in ways we cannot begin to imagine.

In stories of science fiction and inter-galactic travel, there is always the great and terrible question: is there any intelligent life out there? Any intelligent, alien life? The answer is yes. But not in outer space. Intelligent life is lurking in the oceans of planet Earth.

The acrobatics of the humpbacks are as spectacular as their songs. They can leap clear of the water and splash back down again in moments of great excitement at mating time. When you consider that these animals measure up to 16 metres and weigh as much as 60 tons, this is a spectacular sight. (Like most of us, I have only seen this on television: a good thing about modern technology is that brings biophilia straight into your living-room.)

Like all whales, the humpbacks have been persecuted by hunters for centuries. It is reckoned that there were 100,000 humpback whales in the southern hemisphere alone before hunting began; half as many again in the north.

By the 1960s, this had reached a low of 3,000. These whales like coastal waters, and that brings them into contact with humans, which is never a good plan. Humpback whales often become entangled in fishing nets, and, being air-breathers, they drown.

One advantage of the coastal habits of the humpback whale is that it is possible for humans to see them without going to sea for weeks at a time. This makes them tourist attractions, and that makes live humpback whales valuable to humans. In Canada, there are even teams of humans who regularly untangle humpback whales from fishing nets.

Coastal activities of all kinds threaten the humpback: pollution and damage from boats as well as fishing. But the reduction in whale hunting has given the humpback something it has not had for a hundred years and more. It has given it a future.

HUMPBACK WHALE
Scientific name: *Megaptera novaeangliae*
Size: length up to 16 m (52 ft)
weight up to 60 tons
Range: can be found in any ocean in the world
Habitat: ocean
Food: crustaceans, molluscs, fish, krill

67 Vaquita

DOLPHINS and porpoises, the smallest members of the group that includes the great whales, are greatly loved. And very few of the millions of dolphin-lovers have ever seen a real wild one. I have never done so myself: the nearest I got was a series of splashes just visible in my binoculars, off the coast of Indonesia.

But one of the things about biophilia is that you do not need to see every animal in the word in order to feel good about it and want to save it. People are willing to support dolphinkind: not only generously, but selflessly. People who have never seen wild dolphins, and never expect to, will give money and time and support for their beloved dolphins.

Dolphins are among the most loved of all animals. They seem to sparkle with intelligence, and also with innocence. Destruction of dolphins seems particularly hard, particularly wasteful.

The most endangered dolphin is also the smallest, a porpoise called the **vaquita**, which means 'little cow' in Spanish. This is the affectionate nickname given to the animal by the fishermen near the mouth of the Colorado River, in Mexico.

These porpoises are seldom seen now. It's hard to guess how many are left: a few hundred at best. Little is known about them: the animals were unknown to science until 1958. They are tiny by comparison with their relatives, the whales: vaquitas are not much more than 1.2 metres long and weigh little more than 40 kilos. They live in a small area, which gives them the problems of an island species, and that small area is off the coast, which brings them the problems of coastal species. The vaquita is rich in problems.

Vaquitas live around the mouth of the Colorado River. This river has been dammed, which has changed its nature entirely. The daily flood of food from river to sea has been stopped at a stroke. The entire nature of life in the gulf has changed. Furthermore, with human populations and farming along the Colorado River, the river now carries to the sea not food but poisons.

These are complicated problems. The decline of the vaquita could at least be drastically slowed by the control of fishing. It is reckoned that 30 or 40 vaquitas are caught in fishing nets every year, and we know that a small population can't suffer that sort of loss for long. The nets are spread out to catch an endangered species of fish, the totoaba. This fish is now protected and fishing for it is illegal: but totoaba fishing still continues illegally. Laws alone do not save wildlife. Vaquitas are also caught in nets that are put out for other kinds of fish.

There are calls to establish a marine sanctuary in the gulf of the Colorado River: to save a habitat for vaquitas and to create an attractive place for good wildlife tourism. There are also possibilities for establishing a captive breeding population of vaquitas: the animal has never been bred in captivity, so this would be a considerable challenge.

VAQUITA
Scientific name: *Phocoena sinus*
Size: length up to 1.5 m (5 ft)
   weight up to 55 kg (120 lb)
Range: northern Gulf of California, off Mexico
Habitat: sea
Food: fish, squid

68 Leopard

I USED to see leopards every day, more or less. And every time I
saw a leopard, the animal looked more beautiful. In the Luangwa
Valley in Zambia, which for my money is the most beautiful place on
Earth, it is possible to watch leopards at the only time they are truly
busy – at the dead of night.

You can catch one in a powerful spotlight and if – like most of
them – it is not troubled by the light, it is possible to follow and watch
as a leopard goes about its nightly business, which is mostly hunting.

Every time you see a leopard, you are looking at perfection. A
leopard has to be perfect, or it dies. It has no choice. A lion hunting in
a pride, or a dog or a wolf or a hyena living and hunting in a pack,
can afford to take knocks and bangs. As long as it can keep up with
the rest, it will be able to share the kill. But a leopard hunts alone, and
if it is not in perfect condition, it cannot hunt efficiently. You cannot
afford to have a limp when you are chasing animals as alert and as
swift as gazelles. A limping leopard catches nothing. A leopard must
always be at its best: that is why, when you are looking at a leopard,
you are witnessing perfection.

Their beauty was very nearly the end of them. The fur trade paid a high price for a leopard skin. Now the animal is endangered, the trade is illegal: but it still goes on. However, in many places in the world, a person wearing a leopardskin coat is considered a kind of monster. In many places, leopard skins are no longer fashionable.

Animals with such beauty, such power, as leopards will always have the kind of admirer who wants them dead, in order to admire them better. Big game hunting for leopard trophies still takes place.

Leopards are remarkably adaptable animals. They are found throughout Africa south of the Sahara desert, and in much of Asia. If there is food about, the leopard, being smart and canny, will always find a way of making a living. If its natural habitat is taken over by farmland, the leopard is likely to take domestic animals: calves and goats. Because of this, leopards are often poisoned: a poisoned carcass

LEOPARD
Scientific name: *Panthera pardus*
Size: head and body length up to 190 cm (75 in.)
       weight up to 70 kg (155 lb)
Range: Africa south of Sahara, southeast Asia
Habitat: can adapt to any habitat from semi-desert to rainforest
Food: small to medium-sized mammals, birds, insects

is left out for them. The bigger and fiercer the animal, the more likely it is to come up against the people/wildlife clash.

Some estimates say that there are as many as 700,000 leopards in the world. But most experts now agree that this is wildly wrong: that there are less than half that number.

The leopard population is shrinking. But in Africa, and to a lesser extent in Asia, there are wilderness areas set aside as national parks. The Luangwa Valley is just such a place. Leopards and other large mammals may in the end be restricted to such islands. As this begins to happen, more thought and energy must be given to the establishment of wildlife corridors to allow animals to move from park to park.

The fact remains that there are worse places to be marooned than a national park in Africa. As last chances go, Africa has more of them than most places.

69 *Jaguar*

I<small>F</small> spotted cats do not fill you with biophilia, there is not much hope for you. That is why, hot on the heels of the leopard, I am bringing you another spotted cat: very similar, subtly different. And the dangers it faces are in some ways the same, and in some ways quite different.

Here then, is the **jaguar**, the great cat of South America. The leopard is the great secretive cat of Africa and Asia: the night-creeping carnivore that can adapt to many different habitats. The jaguar has many of the same skills. This is the world's third largest cat: only lions and tigers are bigger. A big male jaguar can be reach a length of 1.8 metres.

Jaguars live in all kinds of country. At one time, they lived in the southern US, and were common in most of Central and South America. They are now found in just a few parts of Mexico, and in scattered areas throughout south America as far down as northern Argentina.

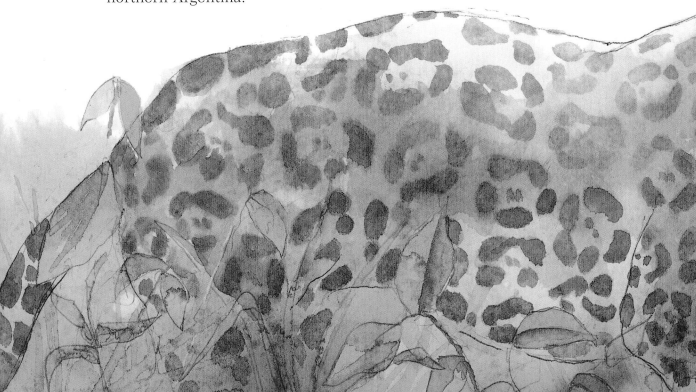

They can make a living anywhere there is wild country and a supply of food: desert, grassland, swamps, open woodland and, best of all, dense rainforest. What they like best is deep forest with plenty of water.

Jaguars like water: they're strong swimmers, and they're good at catching water-living animals, including fish and turtles. They are excellent all-round athletes: they can run and climb trees with great speed and skill. Like leopards, they hunt on their own, in the night, and must live as close as possible to perfection simply to make a living.

We know that all big fierce animals are rare: and that humans have always had a fancy for killing big carnivores. Ever since guns were invented, carnivores have had a hard time: living on the edge of possibility. If you have an especially beautiful coat, like most carnivores, especially those of the cat kind, then you are in still deeper trouble.

The fur craze of the early 1960s sent the price of a jaguar skin soaring, and many animals were killed to please the rich and the stupid. However, really stupid and wasteful killing does, at least, draw the world's attention to a problem. It was at this time that the jaguar became a protected species, and fur coats, especially those made from wild animals, became less fashionable. The jaguar was given the opportunity to begin its recovery from the attacks of the fur trade.

But this chance coincided with the growth of other problems.

JAGUAR
Scientific name: *Panthera onca*
Size: head and body length up to 1.8 m (6 ft)
weight up to 113 kg (250 lb)
Range: South and Central America, Mexico
Habitat: forest, open woodland, swamp, scrub, desert, savannah
Food: mammals, birds

The pace of rainforest destruction, the greatest of all threats, began to gather speed. The jaguars themselves are no longer hunted for their fur: instead, the places where they live are being destroyed. It's all one to the jaguar: either method will wipe them out.

The destruction needs to be halted, and at once. The good news for the jaguar is that there are now national parks in Bolivia, Brazil, Colombia, Peru and Venezuela. It is something.

70 *Malaysian tapir*

DESTRUCTION is not fussy. It takes in all sorts of creatures, all sorts of habitats, from the tops of the mountains to the bottom of the sea. We have, as we make this lightning tour of the animal kingdom, seen how apes and monkeys, whales and porpoises and great cats each suffer from all kinds of deliberate and accidental acts of destruction.

No kind of creature is safe. The beautiful are killed for their beauty: the less beautiful are not let off as the pace of destruction continues. Let us turn to one of the overlooked members of that overcrowded club, the endangered animals of the world. This is the **Malaysian tapir**, a creature of the shadows and thickets of the rainforests of Asia.

It looks a prominent, easily spotted animal, I know, but in the strange, dappled shadows of rainforest, lit by stray shafts of sunlight penetrating the thick canopy far overhead, the tapir's coat merges with the patterns of light and shade and becomes almost invisible.

The Malyasian tapir can grow up to 2.4 metres long and stand over a metre tall at the shoulder. Tapirs are grazing animals. They lie down and hide during the day, coming out at night to graze. They are strong swimmers, and spend a good deal of time underwater.

Direct persecution was just the beginning of the Malysian tapir's problems. Like many big grazers, they're killed for food. They were also considered a nice, exotic trophy, so many of them were killed for something that is curiously called 'sport'. The strangely patterned coat also made it attractive for trophy-hunters and the tapir's skin can be used for especially good leather.

Good news for the animal is that in some of the places where it lives, in Sumatra and Myanmar, the religious beliefs of the local people stop them from killing the tapirs. There are some protected areas of undisturbed forest where the Malaysian tapir can be seen. I have visited one of these, Taman Negar in Malaysia. I spent a very long time staring at shadows, waiting for the wonderfully concealed tapir to appear. I didn't see one: but a night in a rainforest is never wasted.

Rainforests are extraordinary, mysterious places. At night, they are filled with the strangest of noises: a deafening symphony of wildlife. It is thrilling, and it is also rather alarming. A night in rainforest is never wasted, unless, of course, you want to have a good night's sleep. But as you lie there listening, and wondering how many extraordinary creatures are involved in this symphony of the night, you can't help thinking: how could anybody wish to destroy a world such as this? A world so strange, so perfectly unknowable?

MALAYSIAN TAPIR
Scientific name: *Tapirus indicus*
Size: head and body length up to 2.4 m (8 ft)
height at shoulder up to 107 cm (42 in.)
weight up to 300 kg (660 lb)
Range: Sumatra (Indonesia), Malaysia, Myanmar, Thailand
Habitat: tropical forest
Food: plants, especially fresh shoots, fruit

71 African pygmy squirrel

BIG animals are always likely to find trouble. They need a lot of space, for a start, and the humans of this world want more and more space. Big animals often carry a lot of meat, or a lot of fur, which means the hunters are after them.

But one good thing about being a big and spectacular animal is that you can attract the world's attention. Everyone knows what an elephant is: and practically everyone has good feelings about elephants. Most people think that a world without elephants would be a sadder and poorer place to live in.

Conservation organisations have an easier job convincing the world about the large creatures than about the small, the obscure and the ordinary. There are many more little and obscure animals in the world than there are spectacular, headline-grabbing giants. To represent some of the legions of the tiny, the overlooked and the forgotten I have chosen a squirrel. This is consistent with my choices in this lightning sprint through the animal kingdom. I have chosen animals I especially like.

Most of us have a liking for squirrels. Their brightness, their love of activity makes them a delight to watch. They come in many kinds, hundreds of them: tree-climbers, ground-squirrels, and even squirrels that glide from tree to tree, some of the most comic animals I have ever watched.

I have chosen the tiniest squirrel of them all, the **African pygmy squirrel**. It is a little scrap of nothing, feeding off the fungus it finds underneath tree bark.

AFRICAN PYGMY SQUIRREL
Scientific name: *Myosciurus pumilio*
Size: head and body length up to 7.4 cm (2.9 in.)
    tail up to 5.8 cm (2.3 in.)
    weight up to 16.5 g (0.5 oz)
Range: Cameroon, Bioko, Gabon, Nigeria
Habitat: forest
Food: fungus

It weighs a mere 16.5 grams and its head and body are something
between 5.9 and 7.4 centimetres. Its tail is narrow and nearly as
long again.

African pygmy squirrels live in west Africa: Nigeria, Cameroon,
Gabon and Bioko. They are versatile little things, and can make a
living in just about any type of forest. However, just about every type
of forest is under threat.

Because this squirrel is so tiny and so obscure, nobody knows
much about it - how many there are, or what it needs to survive.
Apart from plenty of trees, of course.

There are absolutely no measures in place to protect this species.
No one has noticed it much while it survives, and few will miss it
much if it goes extinct. But these little animals also matter. They
matter just as much as the elephants. They matter, and so do the
forests they live in. We must look after our planet, and look after its
creatures, including those we've never heard of.

72 Brazilian three-toed sloth

WE are mammals. Naturally, of all the groups of animals in the world, we feel closest to mammals. There is some way in which we can begin to understand a chimpanzee, our closest relative. And if we try, we can find some kind of understanding of most mammals.

We can put ourselves in the minds of our pets, our cats and our dogs. We understand when they're happy or sad, when they're hungry or eager for something to do. We can also grasp something of the lives of wild mammals. The social life of the lion isn't like ours; neither, for that matter, is the social life of the elephant. But clever and observant humans have attempted to get inside the minds of these animals and, if we read their books, we, too, can try the same trick.

Out in Africa, following a single pride of lions over a long period, I have felt the first glimmerings of our understanding of lion life. There is a way in which we humans can feel a little of what it is like to be a lion. We are all mammals together, after all.

Naturally, we have a special sympathy for our fellow-mammals: and with that, a feeling that we owe them something. We owe them a world in which they can live, at least. Which brings me to the **Brazilian three-toed sloth**, otherwise known as the maned sloth.

BRAZILIAN THREE-TOED SLOTH
Scientific name: *Bradypus torquatus*
Size: head and body length up to 60 cm (24 in.)
weight up to 6.5 kg (1 lb)
Range: Brazil
Habitat: Atlantic coastal forest
Food: leaves, birds, flowers

What a creature. It is a mammal like us: but it is a beast so strange it might as well come from Mars. We have talked about the cheetah, an animal built for speed. Well, a sloth is built for slowness. Its body works at an extremely slow rate: slow heart, slow digestion and, presumably, slow thoughts.

The advantage of this strange process of slowing down is that the sloth doesn't need to spend its life in ceaseless activity, looking for food. That's the lot of most mammals: a plant-eater needs a lot of plants to survive; a meat-eater must spend a lot of time looking for its single big meal.

But a sloth is very good at just sitting, and better still at simply hanging about. It spends most of its time sitting in the forks of trees, or hanging down from the branches. It's an odd way of living, and a sloth looks utterly bizarre to us humans. The sloth's fur points downwards when it is hanging from a branch: it grows the opposite way from most mammals' fur.

Sloths often look green: algae grows in their fur, which helps them fade into the forest background. They feed at night, mostly on leaves, but they will take small birds if they can find them. They have long claws which help them climb trees. But this odd, slow-moving, slow-living animal can use these claws as weapons to inflict a nasty wound. Its natural enemies are the hunting cats: jaguar and ocelot.

Sloths spend almost all their time in the trees, but occasionally

they come to the ground. They move across the earth with quite desperate slowness. Surprisingly, they can swim pretty well.

I don't need to spell out the dangers for sloths. The Brazilian three-toed sloth lives in the Brazilian coastal forests and practically all of this habitat has now been cleared for agriculture. There are a few reserves left in which they can be found, and there is hope of setting up a few more. No one has managed to keep the animal in captivity. It lives a strange life, remote from human understanding. But of course, if we try to save only the animals we can understand, we'll save precious few. The animal mind is a great unexplored kingdom. It's time we gave more thought to understanding animals, and less to killing them.

73 Long-footed potoroo

IF we don't understand our own small group of mammals, what hope do we have of saving the rest? Once we begin to look beyond the picture-book mammals, the lions and tigers and elephants and zebras, we realise that there are more and more different kinds of mammals, all of them living different lives, and practically all of them in different kinds of danger.

Mammals are one of the five groups of animals that possess backbones - the vertebrates. If we don't understand mammals, then we are seriously struggling to come to terms with the other four groups of vertebrates: the birds, reptiles, amphibians and fish. And if we fail with vertebrates, we can hardly hope to understand the rest: the non-backboned animals, or invertebrates, that include insects, worms, spiders, slugs, jellyfish, sponges, shellfish, and sea squirts: the endless, uncounted and uncountable millions of animals that swarm the modern Earth, facing new human-created dangers every day.

And so, before we leave the mammals on this lightning tour –we shall meet a few more right at the close of this book – I shall finish with a truly obscure one: the **long-footed potoroo**.

This is, without doubt, an excellent name. A potoroo is a marsupial, and looks after its young in a pouch. The most famous of the marsupials is the kangaroo; most of them live in Australasia.

The long-footed potoroo is not a giant, like the big species of kangaroo. It's about 30 centimetres long and its tail is about the same length again. It can travel on two legs or four, and it can, when it needs to, produce a spectacular two-metre jump. It feeds mostly at night, and does so by digging conical pits,

LONG-FOOTED POTOROO

Scientific name: *Potorous longipes*
Size: head and body length up to 42 cm (16.5 in.)
    length of hind foot 10 cm (4 in.)
    tail length 33 cm (13 in.)
    weight up to 2.2 kg (4.9 lb)
Range: Australia
Habitat: riverside vegetation
Food: fungus, other vegetation

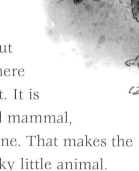

from which it takes fungus, roots and grasses. Humans don't know much about the long-footed potoroo. We don't have clear ideas about where it lives, how many still exist, its precise feeding requirements, or the sort of place it needs in order to survive. It seems to live best in riverside country in Australia, and it probably suffers from the introduced animals, like dogs and foxes, as well as from forest clearance.

Potoroos live in groups or colonies, and 20 of these colonies are known to exist. They are now protected, and new colonies will also be protected if and when they are discovered. There is pressure to protect not just the animals, but the riverside forests as well, which means no more logging. There is also hope of establishing a potoroo colony in captivity.

We don't know a great deal about the long-footed potoroo, but there are moves to try and save it. It is an obscure and overlooked mammal, but something is being done. That makes the long-footed potoroo a lucky little animal.

74 Harpy eagle

IT'S always a great moment when you see a bird of prey: an eagle, a falcon, a hawk, an owl. There are two things that make it especially exciting.

The first is simple enough: they're all stunning to look at. They need to be quite brilliant fliers, or they wouldn't catch anything. For each bird of prey, life depends on the ability to fly superbly.

Birds of prey have different flying skills. It all depends on the kind of animals they catch. Some can hang still in the air, some can fly tremendously fast, some can fly amazingly high, some can fly in perfect silence. They all have one thing in common: whatever form of flight they specialise in, they do it superbly.

The second reason for the excitement is that all birds of prey are rare. As we have seen, it is one of the basic rules of life: big fierce animals are rare. So birds of prey are never going to be common. Even in the best and healthiest of all possible worlds, seeing a bird of prey would still be a special moment.

Which brings us to one of the biggest and most majestic of all the eagles, the **harpy eagle**. This bird is huge, but it is also tremendously agile. Its special skill is to fly through the forest canopy, gliding and jinking through the trees. It has huge feet, which it uses like mechanical grabs. The bird's technique is to glide through the canopy and to take the creatures who live there by surprise, plucking them from their branches in a swift and silent raid.

Harpy eagles live in the forests of South America, and they take monkeys, sloths, porcupines, reptiles and large birds. They are fierce and rather terrible beasts. Even in their prime, these eagles were

HARPY EAGLE
Scientific name: *Harpia harpyja*
Size: length up to 102 cm (40 in.)
weight up to 7 kg (15.5 lb)
Range: Mexico, south to Argentina
Habitat: virgin forest
Food: monkeys, sloths, porcupines, reptiles, birds

never common. Each pair needs an enormous area of forest to call its own. But though they were thin on the ground even in the best of times, they were once found almost all over Central and South America: from Mexico down to the north of Argentina.

They never existed in large numbers, but instead, as successful individuals and pairs. Harpy eagles breed only once every two years, which means that they need to live for a long time to be successful. They live in lowland tropical forest; and the kind of forest they like best is more or less untouched by humans: what is called virgin forest. As before, I do not need to explain further about the greatest threat to their future.

The birds have also been hunted by humans. Because they breed slowly and are naturally spread out, they cannot recover quickly from direct persecution. Harpy eagles are protected by law but, as we know, making a law is one thing: making people keep it, especially in remote and wild places, is quite another.

However, where there is still good forest to be found, there the harpy eagle can be found as well. The harpy eagle can hold its own so long as the remaining bits of rainforest do the same.

Birds of prey, indeed, all the big meat-eating animals, tell us an important truth about the place they live. If a big beast like the harpy eagle can make a living, it means that the forest can provide it with plenty to eat. Therefore there is plenty of life in the forest. When things go wrong, the first animal to suffer is the top predator. So long as we have harpy eagles in South America, it means that there are healthy bits of rainforest left. The harpy eagle is one of this book's many symbols of hope.

75 Usambara eagle owl

Humans are animals of the daylight. We have good eyes, we see in colour, we like light. Darkness and mysteries bother us. In some ways, we are closer to birds than we are to our own group of mammals. Outside the primate group, the group of animals that includes humans, animals do not see colour in the same spectacular way that we do.

Most other mammals live in the world of smell. They use smell to communicate with each other and to understand the world they live in. This is more or less impossible for us to understand: a dog trying to explain smell to us would be like describing colour to a blind person. It has been said that we humans can only smell in black and white. When it comes to smells, a pet dog understands the world better than we can even begin to imagine.

But birds revel in noise and in colour. They sing, they often have bright and gaudy feathers. Birds understand the world through colour and sound: and so do we.

There are many birds in the world: more than 9,000 different species. And birds have found many different ways of making a living. They've even learned to penetrate the darkness. Which brings us to everybody's favourite spooky bird, the owl.

I couldn't resist including another owl. Owls are symbols of mystery, and one of the joys of life is that every wildlife question you can answer opens up an entire new world of mysteries. Every answer brings more and more questions: what could be more wonderful, or more mysterious than that?

The owl I have chosen here is another massive bird of prey: the **Usambara eagle owl**.

USAMBARA EAGLE OWL
Scientific name: *Bubo vosseleri*
Size: length around 65 cm (2 ft)
 weight around 2.5 kg (5 lb)
Range: Tanzania
Habitat: evergreen forest; may be able to survive elsewhere
Food: squirrels, galagos, bats, insects

It lives in the forests of the Usambara mountains in Tanzania, in Africa. What the bird likes best is virgin mountain forest: yet again, I need not explain the main threat to its future.

The Usambara eagle owl is hard to find. It's even possible that it lives in other African forests. A good deal of the Usambara mountain forests were cleared early in the twentieth century, for farmland. It is reckoned that there are now somewhere between 200 and 1,000 Usambara eagle owls left. This has to be a broad estimate because the bird is very hard to trace, and harder still to study.

The future for the Usambara eagle owls, and for the other creatures of the Usambara mountain forests, is in protected areas. Forest reserves have been set up, always an important first step. These areas are protected in law, if not terribly well protected. So the forests need improved protection. It's necessary if this silent, spooky, drifting giant of the Usambara night is to survive.

76 Great bustard

IN a way, size is a definition of wildness: as long as there are big animals about, we know that there is some kind of wildness left on our planet. A very big bird is an especially wonderful sight: and flying birds do not get any bigger than bustards. The bustard family includes the world's largest and heaviest flying bird, the kori bustard, a bird of the African plains. It seems impossible that such an animal should be able to get off the ground, but once in the air its flight is powerful and direct.

Only slightly less enormous, we have a bird that lives on the plains of Europe and northern Asia, and it's one of the most dramatic birds in the world. This is the **great bustard**. A full-grown male can weigh up to 18 kilos. Watching a group of males take off is like watching a fly-past of huge military aircraft: slow, strong, impossibly huge, and utterly majestic. And, of course, deeply wild.

GREAT BUSTARD
Scientific name: *Otis tarda*
Size: weight (males) up to 18 kg (40 lb)
Range: Europe, southern Russia, Ukraine, Mongolia,
China, Turkey, Middle East
Habitat: undeveloped farmland and steppe
Food: plants, invertebrates

There were once great bustards in England, but the last one was shot in the nineteenth century. Shooting and agriculture combined to send the bird extinct in that country, though England was never a great bustard stronghold: the birds prefer the bigger open spaces and drier conditions of the continent.

Great bustards are grassland birds, and they live on insects and seeds. Grasslands, as we know, are always wanted for agriculture. A bird that likes the dry, undeveloped grasslands of the developed world is always going to find life difficult. Grasslands tend to get developed pretty quickly by farmers. This brings the birds into a head-on collision with agriculture, and right to the heart of the people/wildlife clash. This has been the case for a couple of centuries, and the bustard population has got smaller and smaller. It is now down to about 20,000 birds.

But not all the news is glum. Big animals need a lot of space, but they are certainly noticeable. The great bustard is a bird you can't

ignore. It's not going to go extinct by accident. There are conservation measures in place for the birds in many of the countries where they live.

They need protected areas. Great bustards are quite happy to live in farming areas, so long as these areas are not worked absolutely flat out. If farmers can hold back from working their fields while bustards are nesting in them, it's good news for bustards. Why should a farmer do such a thing, when he has a living of his own to make?

Money. That is the simple answer. In Spain, where 8,000 of the world's bustards live, it's possible for farmers to get paid by the government to farm the land more gently. In places where farmers have taken up this scheme, the landscape is lovely and the bird population is dramatic.

In other countries, including Hungary, Germany and Russia, there are protected areas for bustards. When there are bustards around, you can't help but know about them.

77 Purple-backed sunbeam

FROM the largest flying birds to the smallest. There is nothing like a humming-bird. There are about 300 species of humming-birds, most of them in South America: 18 of them go as far north as the US; one or two even reach Canada.

They are, perhaps, the world's flashiest birds. Many of them have spectacular shining feathers, and they can fly in a fashion that dazzles. It's impossible to read any of the figures about humming-bird life without being stunned. Some species can flap their wings 200 times a second, and some can reach speeds of 150 mph for a second or so.

They have, in proportion to their size, the most powerful chest muscles of all birds. They need them for their impossibly swift way of flying. Some species have the longest bills, in proportion to their size, of all birds. The champion is probably the sword-billed humming bird, whose bill is longer than its head and body combined. It uses the bill to dip into long, trumpet-shaped flowers, to drink the nectar.

Humming-birds live at a frantic rate, requiring huge amounts of energy from the rich food of nectar to keep up their extraordinary speed of flight. But they have a very neat way of saving energy. When they sleep at night, they do not doze. They pass into a deep sleep that is more like hibernation than a bird's normal restless sleep.

Their body temperature crashes from around 40˚C to around 20˚C. This energy-saving technique gives the bird a flying start when it begins another high-speed, restless day.

It is always a delight see any humming-bird. Here, I have chosen a bird with the lovely name of **purple-backed sunbeam**.

PURPLE-BACKED SUNBEAM
Scientific name: *Aglaeactis aliciae*
Size: length around 5.2 cm (2 in.)
Range: Peru
Habitat: mountain shrubbery and wooded grassland
Food: nectar

It's impossible to ignore a huge animal like the great bustard: the purple-backed sunbeam is almost the exact opposite. It's next to impossible to see one.

They live only in a small wooded area of the mountains of Peru. It's a hard place to get to, and even if you manage it, it's harder still to find the tiny birds. Just about everything that is known about the purple-backed sunbeam comes from four birds that were shot by scientist-collectors in 1895, and again in 1932. The birds, it was noted, were then fairly common.

An expedition to the area in 1979 confirmed that there were still purple-backed sunbeams to be found there. They were no longer fairly common. And that's about all we know other than the fact that they drink nectar from the bushes of their mountainous homeland.

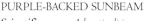

This is a small bird that lives only in a small area. The area is changing, because of the increasing human population. As with island species, habitat destruction is a serious threat, and a small problem is a serious disaster.

Humming-birds are fairly adaptable, however. A number of birds related to the purple-backed sunbeam have managed to work out new ways of life that cope with the changes made by humans. Let us hope that the purple-backed sunbeam can also adapt.

78 Leatherback sea turtle

LET'S continue our journey through the animal kingdom, moving further from our own kind. But we must stay for a while with the backboned animals. We have so far looked only at the mammals (the group that includes humans) and birds. There are five groups of backboned animals altogether: let's turn to the reptiles, and look at the first representative, the **leatherback sea turtle**.

It's a huge animal, the largest of all the sea turtles. It can measure 1.5 metres and can weigh up to 480 kilos. It has weak jaws but that's no problem, because it lives mostly off jellyfish. It also takes a few squid and some fish.

Like the Kemp's ridley sea turtle that we met earlier, the leatherbacks are related to land-living animals. They breathe air and, like all turtles, they must come ashore to lay eggs. That is always the weak point of the turtle's life-cycle. They have to leave the eggs there, on the beach, and return to the sea. Left alone, many of the leatherback sea turtle's eggs are eaten by pigs, crabs and lizards. The tiny turtles, once they have hatched, make their way to the sea, and many more are gobbled up on the way. Life doesn't stop being dangerous when they reach the water: they're often eaten by the small sharks that live near the shore.

LEATHERBACK SEA TURTLE
Scientific name: *Dermochelys coriacea*
Size: length up to 1.5 m (4-9 ft)
     weight up to 480 kg (1,000 lb)
Range: ocean
Habitat: tropical, temperate and sub-polar seas
Food: jellyfish, also squid, fish, algae, crustaceans

The leatherback sea turtle was thought to be very close to extinction back in the 1960s. However, the ocean is full of surprises, and sometimes these are pleasant surprises. Scientists studied the species and worked out that there were more than they had once thought. The numbers are now reckoned to be 100,000 breeding females, which is very encouraging.

Turtles' eggs and the tiny young are very vulnerable to predators. They are very vulnerable indeed to the greediest predator in the world: the human being. Turtle eggs have long been a traditional food of many people. The beaches where the leatherbacks nest have some legal protection, but this isn't enough.

The challenge for conservation is to manage the collecting of turtle eggs in a way that safeguards some of them. That would be good news for the people who eat turtle eggs; and good news for the turtles. We are back to the tragedy of the commons, and the deep and difficult problems of sharing. There is already a scheme in Malaysia for hatching leatherback eggs - a very difficult and troublesome process. The scheme could work out to be of long-term benefit to both people and turtles.

There are other problems facing the leatherbacks. A particularly unpleasant one is the rubbish thrown from ships and washed out from land. Turtles often mistake floating plastic bags for jellyfish. They eat them, but they cannot digest plastic, and so they die. Turtles also drown when they are caught in fishing-nets.

The good news is that there are very many more leatherback turtles than was once feared. The bad news is that there are very many more threats to them than there were before.

79 Cook Strait tuatara

REPTILES were once the dominant group of large animals on Earth. Dinosaurs, the giant reptiles that died out 65 million years ago, fascinated us all at some stage in our lives. Some people believe that dinosaurmania is a phase we go through: something we grow out of. But if we are wise, we keep this fascination with us for ever.

For some people, dinosaurs are the love and the work of a grown-up lifetime. But for most of us, dinosaurs merely open the door. They show us the endless possibilities of life: how many different kinds of strange and wonderful (and ferocious) creatures the world can come up with.

And dinosaurs also tell us about the endless fragility of life. If a creature as huge and as fierce as Tyrannosaurus rex can go extinct, well, so can anything. And that, of course, is what this book is all about.

There are plenty of modern reptiles left, and they are not ridiculous, lumbering throwbacks that are hanging on by the skin of their teeth. But reptiles teach us that life is infinitely precarious. There is something about every reptile on Earth that whispers: remember the dinosaurs?

That is why, for a second reptile in this lightning sprint, I have chosen the **Cook Strait tuatara**. Few things look more prehistoric than this strange reptile. And for a very good reason: like the coelacanth, the Cook Strait tuatara is one of those 'living fossils'.

Tuataras belong to the order of *Sphenodontia*, sometimes called beakheads. They are not dinosaurs, but there were many different species of beakheads that lived at the same time as the dinosaurs. Now there is just the one species left. Scientists are not sure if it has survived unchanged for all this time, or whether this is a new species, a modern development from an ancient order. Either way, the animal is perfectly capable of making its living in the modern world. It used to live on the main islands of New Zealand, but for the last 150 years it has only been able to keep going on some of the small islands off the New Zealand coast. It is found on 29 of them altogether.

Tuataras live in the burrows dug by the seabirds that nest on the islands, the shearwaters and petrels. Bird and reptile often share the same burrow. This unusual arrangement works very well. The problem, however, is rats. These animals were introduced – though, of course, accidentally – by humans. Scientists are investigating how much and what kind of damage the rats do to the tuataras.

The islands themselves all have some kind of protection by law. They are official nature reserves, and visits are limited and controlled. All this is good news for the tuatara. Its weirdness, its status as a 'living fossil' makes people want to save it. After all, the beakheads have been around for 200 million years. Figures like that deserve to be respected. Two hundred million years of life really should not be wiped out by accident.

COOK STRAIT TUATARA
Scientific name: *Sphenodon punctatus*
Size: (males) up to 60 cm (24 in.)
weight (males) up to 1.2 kg (2.6 lb)
Range: New Zealand
Habitat: rocky islands
Food: invertebrates, birds' eggs, lizards, frogs

80 Malabar tree toad

Endless forms most beautiful.' We met these four words earlier in this book. They also appear at the end of one of the most important books ever written, Charles Darwin's *On The Origin of Species*. And the more you look at the animal kingdom, the harder it is to believe what you see. The fact that many animals are beautiful is perhaps the least surprising thing of all. It is not the beauty that amazes so much as the endlessness of the forms.

Endless? Well, try this. Have a guess: how many different species of frogs and toads do you think there are alive in the world today? A dozen? A hundred? More: five hundred? Go mad: how about a thousand? Still not enough. There are about 2,700 different kinds that we know about: firebellies, spadefoots, bullfrogs, leopard frogs, true frogs, poisonous frogs, narrow-mouthed toads, and on and on. Almost endlessly.

Darwin said that the beautiful forms were endless for a very good reason. Time, nature and the world produce new species. Over millions of years, the world and its creatures change and change again. So long as the world continues without ending, so the number of forms of animals that live there will continue to change, unendingly.

This is evolution, and it happens all the time. What humans have done is to change the rules of the game. The violent changes humans have made to the Earth have changed the way in which life works. An extraordinary number of animals have gone extinct in the last few thousand years; a still more extraordinary number now live under the threat of extinction.

This affects, as we have seen, every different kind of habitat;

and now, as we continue our sprint, we see that it affects every different group of animals as well. We will now touch briefly on the amphibians, and salute the **Malabar tree toad.**

The toad was first discovered more than a hundred years ago, and it lives in Kerala, in southern India. Once it had been discovered, nobody really thought much about it again until quite recently. By this time, most of the hot, wet forest of Kerala had been chopped down. It was assumed that the Malabar tree toad had gone extinct: the fate that threatened so many animals that live in the world's hot, wet forests.

But in 1982, a single specimen was discovered, and a few years later, several more turned up. The Malabar tree toad is hanging on. The good news is that that the few bits of Kerala forest left now have some kind of protection. The habit of felling enormous areas of forest to make farmland has been stopped.

Amphibians are strange animals, the fourth group of backboned animals. All life began in the water; the amphibians were the first group of backboned animals to leave the water and try life on dry land. They paved the way for all the other groups that were to follow. In a way, we owe amphibians a debt we can never repay. The best thing we can do for them is to let them be. Or – to be more practical and purposeful – to look after the areas in which they live and, most importantly, to preserve such bits of hot, wet forest as we have left, to allow the amphibians, all the frogs and toads to continue to be, and continue to become, endless forms most beautiful.

MALABAR TREE TOAD
Scientific name: *Pedostibes tuberculosa*
Size: up to 3.5 cm (1.3 in.)
Range: India
Habitat: wet forest
Food: invertebrates

81 Great hammerhead shark

'ER, I don't know. Sorry, I really have no idea.' Not, I think you will agree, the most helpful sort of answer. But an awful lot of questions about the ocean, home to the fifth group of backboned animals, are best answered with an 'er-I-don't-know'. The oceans are too big, too deep, too difficult: hard places to learn in. Human knowledge of the oceans really is very shallow indeed. So let us look at the **great hammerhead shark**, otherwise known as the er-I-don't-know fish.

There are two main groups of fish, four groups altogether. We shall stop first at cartilaginous fish, a group which includes 600 species of sharks, rays and skates. We have already looked at and marvelled at the biodiversity of the sharks, but no harm to marvel again.

Sharks have no swim-bladders. That means they cannot hang motionless in the water, like goldfish in a bowl. For most sharks, life is about moving forward: and that is true of the great hammerhead. There are nine species of hammerhead altogether, and naturally I have chosen the biggest and most spectacular, the great hammerhead, which can measure up to 4.6 metres long. Great hammerheads have been known to attack swimming humans.

The question everyone who looks at hammerheads has to ask is this: why is its head such a peculiar shape? And the answer is: 'Er, I don't know.' The eyes and the nostrils are placed as far apart as possible, right at the tips of that extraordinary head. Why? Scientists have not come up with a convincing answer.

GREAT HAMMERHEAD SHARK
Scientific name: *Sphyrna mokarran*
Size: length up to 4.6 m (15 ft)
Range: ocean
Habitat: ocean
Food: fish

'Er, I don't know,' seems like a pretty feeble response. And it is a response science often comes up with. This is not to say that science and scientists are feeble: it is to say that life is more bewildering, more weird, more wonderful than humans can understand, and the weirdness of its animals is something that not even the finest human brains in the world can explain.

Hammerheads are found in most of the oceans of the world, and different species can cope with different conditions: some prefer deeper water, others prefer to be closer to the coast, some like warmer water, others colder. The great hammerhead mostly prefers the shoreline, and fairly shallow water.

So how many great hammerheads are left? Er, I don't know. What sort of danger are they in? How much chance have they got? What are the main threats? What must we do to make sure they can survive? I don't know, I don't know, I don't know.

We live in a world full of mysteries: the more we find out, the more questions we want to ask. It is, though, a trifle shocking to learn that such a big animal can exist, and that no one has a clue about it. Not even the most obvious question can be answered.

Again, this is not to say how stupid humans are: but how wonderful life is. We may not know much about the great hammerhead, but we can at least revel in it. We may not be able to answer the questions, but we can enjoy the mystery. Humans can be arrogant creatures: and sometimes people like to speak as if we knew everything. Once we start looking closely, however, we can see that when it comes to learning about the world, we have only just begun. And seeking to find out just a little bit more is one of the greatest and noblest tasks a person can do. Understanding the world, you see, is a part of saving the world.

82 Devil's Hole pupfish

ONE last backboned animal before we move into the teeming masses of the backboneless billions. But there are enough fish to do a fair amount of teeming on their own. There are four main groups of fish: the shark's group; the two smaller groups containing creatures called lampreys and hagfish; and the biggest group, the bony fish.

There is enough biodiversity among fish to last lifetime after lifetime of study; there are something like 25,000 species of fish known to science. We shall touch briefly on the **Devil's Hole pupfish**.

These are members of a group of tiny bony fish. There are about 35 different kinds – and all of them are in danger. They measure between 2 centimetres and 7.5 centimetres. They are pretty easy to overlook. The different species are found in different habitats in the southern US and Mexico.

The name of Devil's Hole pupfish is sometimes given to the members of the group that live in fresh waters in or around a cave formation called Devil's Hole; I'm talking about a single species, *Cyprinodon diabolis*. This species is found only on a small shelf of rocks in the cave. Back, yet again, to the question of island species. With such a tiny part of the world as its home, the Devil's Hole pupfish is in the usual situation: a small disaster would be a total catastrophe.

Other pupfish are vulnerable in the same sort of way. One species is found only in ten springs, another only in six small springs near to Devil's Hole.

DEVIL'S HOLE PUPFISH
Scientific name: Cyprinodon diabolis
Size: Cyprinodom species vary between 2 cm
(0.8 in.) to 7.5 cm (3 in.)
Range: US, Mexico
Habitat: springs
Food: Cyprinodom species exploit various different food
sources; Cyprinodon diabolis feeds only on algae

Our own chosen species, the Devil's Hole pupfish, is not really much of a devil – not compared with the great hammerhead shark. It lives entirely on blue-green algae, plant-like bacteria that grow on the rocks of its home, the single rocky shelf.

Like many species, the pupfish are, in a way, victims of their own success. They have been successful in terms of biodiversity: in their ability to change into many and different forms. They have been successful in adapting very cleverly indeed to a very small area. They are specialists: our blue-green algae feeder is an extreme specialist. It is so specialised, it cannot change its mind and live in another way. Its own success has driven it into a corner. Once again, we meet the tender trap of specialisation.

Once animals like the Devil's Hole pupfish have become specialists, they can cope with anything except a change in the conditions they have adapted for. And humans are always changing things: altering the world for their convenience, for some passing whim.

The different pupfish species are threatened by change. Often these are changes in the water level, or in the water quality, as humans take water for their homes and for industries and for farming. Humans have also introduced other animals to the pupfish's waters, which again, change the conditions the pupfish have adapted for. Mosquito fish, crayfish, bullfrogs, large-mouthed bass and snails have all been introduced, and they change the way the habitat works. The extreme specialist feels the pinch. The tender trap closes in.

Research is being done into the lives and ways of this group of obscure and unspectacular animals. There are also the beginnings of a captive breeding programme. What is necessary, however, is the removal of the introduced species, and the restoration of the water levels. If this isn't done, a small part of the Earth's biodiversity will be stamped out.

83 Iowa Pleistocene snail

NOW we move into the backboneless animals, the invertebrates, and life gets complicated. Well, life is always a complicated business, as we have seen. But the numbers and the endless forms of the backboneless animals are almost impossible to understand.

Most of the animals in this book are from the backboned group and, of these, a good few are birds, and most of the rest are mammals. I have brought in animals of other kinds, but mammals dominate our minds. Why not? We are mammals ourselves.

Mammals are, as we know, just one of the five groups of the world's backboned animals. This larger group, to which all backboned animals belong, is a phylum: we humans belong to the phylum of chordates.

There is not one single phylum of backboneless animals. Backboneless animals come in endless forms. There are 32 different phyla. Each group is more different from the other than a human is from a Devil's Hole pupfish.

I don't have the space to give each phylum a chapter to itself. The backboneless beasts that follow in our lightning sprint will just have to stand for all the uncountable hordes of them: a handful of creatures must do for the endless forms.

We shall turn first to the phylum of molluscs, a group that includes squids and shellfish. There are about 50,000 species in this group, a dizzying enough number to start with. And of these, 40,000 are of the slug and snail kind. So to represent endangered molluscs, let us turn to the **Iowa Pleistocene snail**.

This is a tiny snail found in only 18 places in the US; 17 of them, as you would expect, in Iowa. The animal measures only 8 millimetres. It is not really an animal likely to be the cause of much attention.

And yet this is a happy story: of people who are prepared to put themselves out in order to save a tiny mollusc – one that nobody would miss.

The Iowa Pleistocene snail has a lot in common with the Devil's Hole pupfish: it lives off algae, and it has fallen into the tender trap of specialisation. It is found only in and around the entrances to caves, caves which must have a permanent, or near-permanent, supply of ice. These animals like wet and cold. In the Ice Age (during a period of history called the Pleistocene), when much of the Earth was covered in ice, snails such as this were plentiful; now, in warmer times, the snail has found a series of small places where it can hang on and make a living.

All was going well enough until it came into contact with humans. As a matter of fact, I could write that sentence about almost every animal in this book. With the Iowa Pleistocene snail, this happened about 150 years ago. Humans needed to get rocks and stones from the earth, to build houses and roads, and they needed to turn wilderness into farmland. And that destroyed most of the places where the Iowa Pleistocene snail was able to live its strange life.

But a few years ago, the people who own the land where the snails survived were asked to look after the few remaining scraps of its habitat. And two-thirds of them agreed. This has stopped immediate fears of extinction: meanwhile, conservation organisations are hoping to buy some of the snail habitat, which would keep the land and the snails safe for the immediate future.

IOWA PLEISTOCENE SNAIL
Scientific name: *Discus macclintocki*
Size: width around 8 mm (0.3 in.)
Range: US
Habitat: cave entrances
Food: tree leaves

84 Giant clam

FROM a tiny mollusc to a giant: one of the most spectacular of all living creatures. And if you don't believe a mollusc can be spectacular, then it's time you learned about the **giant clam**.

In fact, there are nine species of giant clams, and all of them are in danger. But let us turn to the biggest of the lot, *Tridacna gigas*. It's the world's largest shelled mollusc, and it can weigh more than 200 kilos. Most of the weight is shell, but the living tissue can still weigh as much as 65 kilos. It can measure up to 137 centimetres in length.

It can live for up to 100 years. It lives this long life in one place, and it feeds on plankton, the tiny scraps of life that are found drifting through the seas. This is the same diet, the same minute items that the great whales live on. These two giants of the sea live on almost invisible specks.

GIANT CLAM
Scientific name: *Tridacna gigas*
Size: shell length up to 137 cm (53.9 in.)
weight up to 200 kg (440 lb)
Range: Indo-Pacific Ocean
Food: plankton

But the giant clams know another life before they select the place where they sit down and rest for a century. Like butterflies and frogs, the clams live their early life in a shape and manner quite different from the one they will take on when they are grown up. They hatch from eggs into the form of free-swimming shelled animals, but they live the free life for just a few days. In some species it is reckoned to be no more than nine days: perhaps even less than that. They then seek a permanent resting spot, and there they sit, eating plankton, looking spectacular. They live these long and strange lives in the Indian and the Pacific oceans, and they prefer coastal waters. This inevitably brings them into contact with humans and many of the problems of the coastal life we have already explored. The biggest clam of them all, our own *Tridacna gigas* is found near the Philippines, and across to the group of little Pacific islands known as Micronesia.

The problem for giant clams is obvious: they are very large pieces of food that don't even try to run away. Any kind of serious commercial fishing will soon send the population crashing. For example, the fishermen of Fiji took out 50 tons of their own giant clam species in the space of nine years. This is simply fishing for extinction. There is also a trade in the shells of giant clams, and the living animals are bought up by people who keep aquariums.

The only real solution to the problems of the giant clams is a control on fishing. This brings us back to the tragedy of the commons. There has been talk of breeding the clams in captivity, and then bringing them back to the wild. This always sounds like a good idea but, so far, the released clams have all died.

Protecting clams is a difficult problem. But if there are to be clams in the future – whether as food for humans, income for fishermen or for the sake of the strangeness and beauty of the clams themselves – it's a problem that has to be taken very seriously, and dealt with immediately.

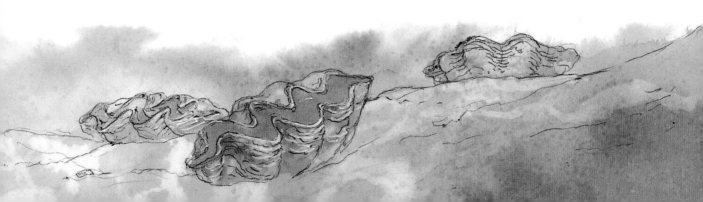

85 Wetapunga

ANY conservation book has to be full of problems – but it must also be a celebration of life. And if we are to celebrate life, then the thing to celebrate is the extraordinary number of ways there are of living; the extraordinary numbers of shapes and forms and fashions in which it is possible for animals to live. If we are to celebrate life, we must celebrate biodiversity.

And if we are to save life on Earth, we must do so, not by selecting a few favourites, the cuddly and the lovely and the spectacular; we must seek to save the lot of them. Life is worth saving; therefore, it is worth saving life in every form in which it appears on earth: the endless forms most beautiful.

And so, as we celebrate biodiversity towards the end of this madcap sprint through the animal kingdom, I make no apologies for stopping and bringing you five animals all of the same kind. This is because the best way to celebrate biodiversity is to look at the insects. There are, after all, something like 750,000 different kinds of them. Not counting, of course, the species that are unknown to science.

Endless forms, certainly: but most beautiful? It's all in the way you look at a thing, I know, but many people would find it hard to love a **wetapunga**. This is the heaviest insect in the world: a big female can weigh up to 72 grams. She can also be up to 10 centimetres long.

WETAPUNGA
Scientific name: *Deinacrida heteracantha*
Size: length up to 100 mm (4 in.)
  length including legs up to 178 mm (7 in.)
Range: New Zealand
Habitat: forest
Food: leaves, occasionally dead invertebrates

There are 11 species of weta, and for the many of us who are wary of insects, the weta is a walking nightmare. It does most of its living by night, too, coming out at dusk to feed on leaves.

Wetas live in the islands around New Zealand – so we can already guess that this is a classic story of humans moving the evolutionary goalposts. As we know, the only mammals in New Zealand were, at one time, bats. Then came humans, bringing with them cats, rats, possums, pigs and deer. They also brought their axes, changing the shape of the land, cutting down the forests.

The wetas were wiped out on the mainland. These days, they hang on in the outer islands but, even here, there are introduced predators. The wetapunga now lives only on Little Barrier Island. Here, the wild population of cats was wiped out, but without the cats, there were more rats than ever before. Once you start messing about with nature, there's no end to your problems.

Wetas are insects that grew to a giant size because of the lack of mammal predators. When humans brought in their predators, the weta found that it was too huge and too strong for its own good. A weta is easy to find, and a lot to eat.

But the offshore islands are still places where the different species of weta can live. Given a fair and mammal-free run at things, the wetas can re-establish themselves. In 1976, 43 wetas of a single species – the St Stephen Island giant weta – were released onto Maud Island. There are now many thousands of them. If only it could always be like that for every endangered species. If only it was always that easy – but at least, there are now reserves for wetas on other islands that are managed by conservationists. These spectacular and alarming creatures have been given a second chance.

seen, the beauty is not always obvious. As we continue to look

86 Pygmy hog sucking louse

LIFE comes in endless forms most beautiful. But as we have
seen, the beauty is not always obvious. As we continue to look
at the insect group, we might think that life comes in endless forms
most horrible.

What insects do I hate the most? If mosquitoes irritate you, then
the tiny sweat bees that live in the mopane trees of Africa and which
gather in large numbers around your eyes, nose and mouth would
drive you insane. Some of the aggressive African bees – those that
defend their nests with such spectacular bravery – are seriously
painful (I speak with personal knowledge here) and they can kill you,
if enough of them manage to sting you.

The tsetse fly of Africa passes on diseases to cattle in a bite that is
incidentally very painful to humans. (In some areas, it also transmits
a disease that kills humans.) Where there are many tsetse flies, you
cannot start cattle farming. It happens that most of the great game
parks of Africa are places where the tsetse fly is found: places where
it is impossible to farm. That is why they have been left wild. We have
the horrible tsetse fly to thank for some of the most beautiful places
left on the planet.

So there is good news to be found from beasts we might consider
horrible. Life is found in all manner of shapes and forms, and if some of
the forms seem nasty to us humans: well, we must just rise above it.

Which brings us to an animal, a rather horrible animal,
called the **pygmy hog sucking louse**. This is a parasite: it
lives off the blood of an animal called the pygmy hog.
Nobody knows much about the pygmy hog sucking
louse; nobody likes it much either. Certainly not
pygmy hogs.

These are small wild pigs that live in two small areas of India. The pygmy hog is itself very close to extinction. Hunting has killed many of the hogs; and now the destruction of the grasslands where it lives bring extinction ever closer.

Extinction is not just a personal matter for a single species. Extinction is also possible disaster for other species. This is because all life is connected. The grasslands themselves could not exist without grazing animals: all the grassland insects, for example, not to mention the grasses themselves, depend on the grazing animals, just as the grazing animals depend on the grasses. The grassland predators depend on the grazers for food; therefore, they too depend on the grasses. Everything links up: that is what life is all about.

The pygmy hog sucking louse is a parasite. Without its host species, it has no existence. If the pygmy hog goes, the pygmy hog sucking louse goes with it. If the two small wildlife sanctuaries of Manas and Barnadi can be saved, then it is likely that the pygmy hog will hang on. And therefore the pygmy hog sucking louse will hang on as well.

No species is an island. Different forms of life connect. Looking after a single species will also protect a vast number of others: most of them tiny, easily missed things like insects, like parasites. Running a species into extinction will sends ripples of trouble throughout its neighbours. All life is connected. So is all death.

PYGMY HOG SUCKING LOUSE
Scientific name: *Haematopinus oliveri*
Size: (females) up to 4.2 mm (0.16 in.)
Range: India
Habitat: pygmy hogs
Food: blood of pygmy hogs

87 Large blue butterfly

EVERYBODY likes butterflies: so much so that we hardly even think of them as insects. But insects they most certainly are, their lives stranger and more complex than we can understand. And when it comes to endless forms most beautiful, there is not a single group in the world that shows this better. There are something like 100,000 species of butterflies and moths, not counting, of course, those that are still unknown to science.

We talked in the last chapter about the way one form of life depends on another form of life. Few animals show us this idea more clearly than the **large blue butterfly**. There are five species of large blue butterfly, all of them in danger; we shall concentrate mainly on the one with the scientific name of *Maculinea arion*. It has already gone extinct in Britain.

Butterflies live their lives in four distinct stages: first an egg, then a caterpillar, then a pupa, the still period in which the caterpillar makes its great change to its final form – the full-winged and gorgeous butterfly.

The caterpillars of the large blue eat the flowers on which they are born. The species each have different plants they lay their eggs on: not just any plant will do. Then the caterpillars fall to the ground – and there they wait to picked up by an ant. Not just any ant will do, either: the caterpillars have to run up against one of the ants from the group called *Myrmica*.

The caterpillar leaks out a liquid that these particular ants happen to like very much. So the ants carry the caterpillars to their underground nests, and there, they look after the caterpillars as if they were domestic cows. They milk them for the liquid, which has the pleasant name of honeydew.

LARGE BLUE BUTTERFLY
Scientific name: *Maculinea arion*
Size: wing span up to 45 mm (1.8 in.)
Range: western Europe to southern Siberia,
Armenia, Mongolia, China
Habitat: anywhere where host plant and host ant species
occur in close proximity
Food: flowering head of host plant (caterpillars);
nectar (adult butterflies)

The caterpillars spend the winter in the ants' nest, safe from harm, from enemies and from the cold. Then, still underground, the caterpillar turns into a pupa and four weeks later, it has become a large blue butterfly. It creeps to the surface, spreads out its large blue wings, and flies away.

This way of living together benefits both species involved in the arrangement. The ants get the honeydew, the caterpillars get the protection. It is called symbiosis. It's a very effective way of living: but it's complicated. There is a lot that can go wrong. And once humans start shifting the goalposts, disasters follow.

Large blue butterflies can't live without the plants the caterpillars live on, and they can't live without the ants. These two things are generally found on land that hasn't been developed very much. Once farmers start improving the grassland with weed-killers and fertilisers or, worse still, ploughing up the grassland for growing crops, then the complicated relationship between plant, ant and butterfly is broken. And it cannot be mended.

There has been concern about the large blue butterfly for many years. It has never been a common species, as you would expect from its complicated life. The drastic changes in the countryside of Britain and the rest of Europe in the second half of the twentieth century pushed the large blue butterfly into rarity. As the butterfly grew rarer, so conservationists tried to save it in Britain. They were too late.

All species of large blue butterfly are found in isolated groups in the north of Europe and Asia. They will continue to hang on – so long as there are wild places left for them.

88 American burying beetle

THERE was a great scientist called J.B.S. Haldane. He was once asked what his lifelong study of the natural world had told him about the nature of the creator of the universe. What was the most obvious characteristic of the creator? Haldane thought for a moment, and then answered: 'An inordinate fondness for beetles.'

Of the total number of species of animals known to science – the best estimate available has it at 1,032,000 species – almost one third are beetles. There are 290,000 species of beetles known to crawl about the Earth today, and no one can say how many more there are that are unknown to science.

If you want to understand the impossible complexity of life on Earth, then start counting beetles. Beetles baffle the brain; beetles dizzy human understanding. Charles Darwin, whom we have met before in this book, was not only one of the greatest scientists that ever lived – perhaps *the* greatest – he was also, when young, absolutely mad about beetles.

He collected them crazily, obsessively. It was a fashionable thing to do, among a very few fanatical people, much as the extreme form of birdwatching – the chasing of rarities – is today. And in some ways, this mad collecting is silly. But it was one of the many things that prepared Darwin for his great understanding about evolution: Darwin was the man who told us how life works.

And if ever there was a group of animals that tells us about endless forms, it is the beetles. So let us turn to an endangered beetle and, as we do so, celebrate not only the bewildering numbers of beetles, but the entire complexity of life on Earth. Let us turn to the **American burying beetle**.

This beetle – this species and its very close relatives – is the only beetle in the world that looks after its young. Most beetles, like most insects, lay their eggs and that is an end to the matter.

But the American burying beetle first finds a corpse: a dead animal, one of the backboned group, a small rodent or a small bird. A male and female beetle find such a carcass, and they bury it in the soil. This is quite a task for a beetle. Once they have the dead animal below ground, they trim off the fur or the feathers, and roll the dead animal up into a ball. They then cover it with liquids from their own bodies: this slows down the speed at which the body rots. This is a fairly grisly tale, I know: but life is not all about the prettiness of large blue butterflies.

The female then lays her eggs underground, and these then hatch into larvae, or grubs. Like butterflies, beetles pass through four stages in their life. The larvae are fed on liquids from the corpse. The parents look after them until they turn into pupae. The beetles even have a method of talking to their young: they make a sound that is certainly used as an alarm call, to warn the grubs of dangers, and which may be used for other kinds of communication.

It's hard to tell whether this is a touching story of parental care, or a horrible story of corpse-eating. Whichever way you look at it, it's life. The American burying beetle was once common over much of north America. It's not exactly clear why the numbers have fallen away. But the main reason is probably that there are fewer small animals for them to bury. And this is a very large problem indeed: not one that can be solved overnight. There is, in short, less life around. Less variety.

AMERICAN BURYING BEETLE
Scientific name: *Nicrophorus americanus*
Size: length up to 36 mm (1.4 in.)
Range: Canada, US
Habitat: mature forest, pasture, shrub thickets
Food: carrion

89 Columbia River tiger beetle

I THOUGHT long and hard about the best way to finish this
journey through the animal kingdom: which animal to place at
the far end of this sprint through the endless forms most beautiful.
And I really feel that we could not do better than another beetle.

A tiger allows us to understand the glory of life. You cannot think
of tigers without a feeling of awe. But animal life is not just about the
superstars of the animal kingdom. We must try and understand not
only the glory of life but also its perfectly glorious complexity. One
beetle makes this point: another beetle rams it home. Do you realise
that if I gave an account of every single species of beetle in the world,
this book would be nearly a million pages long? With just two beetles
in the whole book, I'm letting you off lightly.

So let us turn, not to the tiger, but to the **Columbia River tiger
beetle**. A small animal, yet another small animal, with a small part to
play in its own habitat. We have seen how plants and animals depend on
each other. There comes the terrible question:
how many extinctions can we afford?
The answer is best understood by
something called the rivet-popper
hypothesis. Each species of animal plays a
small part in its own habitat: small but
significant. In the same way, a jet-plane
is held together with rivets, and each
rivet plays a small but significant part

COLUMBIA RIVER TIGER BEETLE
Scientific name: *Cicindela columbica*
Size: length: up to 12 mm (0.5 in.)
Range: US
Habitat: sand dunes, river sandbanks
Food: small insects

226

in stopping the plane from falling apart. Now it hardly matters to the passengers in a jet-plane if the plane loses a rivet here and a rivet there. But if there comes a point when too many rivets are lost, the wings will fall off in mid-air.

That's what's happening to the planet; to every habitat on Earth. One small extinction follows another: somehow, the habitat keeps on going. But with every extinction, the Earth is getting weaker.

It's clear that the large number of species on the planet is no mere happy accident. This is the way in which the planet works. Biodiversity is how life on Earth manages. With less diversity, life becomes a weaker thing. The rivets keep popping: with every lost rivet, the danger increases.

The Columbia River tiger beetle is just another small part in the life of the planet. It was once found in fairly large numbers on the banks of three of the rivers of the US: the Snake, the Columbia and the Salmon. It now lives at only 14 places on the Salmon.

The problem was simple: the construction of dams changed the rivers for ever. It changed the nature of the banks, the way the river works, the way in which animals could make a living in the river and beside it. The Columbia River tiger beetle is a hunting beetle that

lives on the banks. The larvae live in burrows, and attack passing insects for food The adult is an active, scurrying hunter. The damming of the river simply took away its banks.

The Columbia River tiger beetle has been wiped out over most of its range, including the Columbia River. But at least the remaining habitat has now been protected. No further dam, it has been announced, will be built on the Salmon River: so the beetle and the beetle's habitat is safe for the time being.

This is in a small way, cheering. Now let us look at more cheering things. We have looked so far at 89 animals. Some of these have been good news stories: many of the stories have been jam-packed with bad news. Every habitat is in danger, we have seen that. Now, as we conclude this sprint through the animal kingdom, we are forced to the conclusion that every group of animals is in danger as well: the backboned kinds, in their five different forms, the backboneless ones, including the teeming hordes of insects, the uncountable beetles.

There are times when conservation seems hopeless: when it seems that the only thing to do is give up. But giving up is the worst crime of all in conservation. And so let us move onto the next ten animals: ten animals that will, I hope, cheer us all up and fill us full of hope.

90 Giant panda

SOMETIMES it seems that conservation is nothing but gloom and doom. But there's more to conservation than misery. That's why, as we move into the nineties of this one hundred-strong bestiary, I will bring you ten animals to cheer about; ten animals to cheer you up. If you ever start to feel gloomy and doomy about the animals that live on the planet, reach for this book and turn to the nineties.

These ten good-news stories are not here to fool you into thinking that everything is perfect, that there is nothing but jollity for all of life on Earth. But if you have kept with me on our journey as far as number 90, you already know that. You know there is good news and there is bad news: and that it's our job to try and turn the bad news into good. And at the same time, when we do come across a bit of good news, I think we are entitled to cheer.

The first hurrah I have chosen is the **giant panda**. This is probably the most recognisable animal on Earth; it is also everybody's favourite endangered animal. It was one of the first animals that people really started to worry about: it was the animal right at the beginning of the conservation movement. It is the symbol of the Worldwide Fund for Nature, a conservation organisation that was of special help to me as I wrote this book.

It isn't that pandas have stopped being endangered, or that it's safe to stop worrying about them. The amazing thing about the panda is that it has survived at all. It lives in China, the most crowded country on Earth. It lives in the forest. Its skin is worth a fortune. Everyone wants the land it lives on and the skin off its back as well. Nor does its own country have the most brilliant record in the world on conservation. But the panda hangs on. The Chinese government continues to support panda conservation. There are already 13 panda reserves in China, and this number could double in the next few years to protect nearly two-thirds of the world's wild pandas.

There are probably between 800 and 1,000 pandas left. The destruction of the hill-forest where they live has now been stopped. This is good news for the pandas: and also for preventing the terrible floods that some areas have suffered. Future plans include 'wildlife corridors' which will allow the pandas to travel from reserve to reserve.

The reserves protect more than giant pandas. They also hold the delightful red panda, various cats including the snow leopard, various deer, the golden monkey, and a weird animal that looks like a golden cow with a goat's head, called the tarkin. There are also some spectacular birds, including many different species of pheasant.

There are problems; of course there are problems. The main one is protection: the reserves need more people to stop poachers going in there and killing the animals for food, fur and for Chinese medicine. But at least the Chinese government wants the panda to survive. And amazingly, the panda is doing just that.

Hurrah.

GIANT PANDA
Scientific name: *Ailuropoda melanoleuca*
Size: length up to 1.5 m (5 ft)
weight up to 150 kg (330 lb)
Range: China
Habitat: forest with bamboo understorey
Food: bamboo; also grass, bulbs, insects, rodents

91 Marsh harrier

I NEVER thought I'd see one. It was extinct in Britain, you see. It was a bird that made people give up hope. And now, I have seen hundreds. In fact, I can go for a walk every day at the right time of year, and I see one every time. Isn't that something worth cheering?

The bird is the **marsh harrier**, and it's a real success story. The marsh harrier is a bird of prey. All birds of prey have their own special flying tricks, which they use to catch the animals they eat. The marsh harrier's secret is to fly very, very slowly. This is much harder than it sounds: if any flying thing, machine or bird or insect or bat, flies too slowly, then it simply falls out of the air. The marsh harrier's talent is to fly very slowly indeed without falling. It uses its slow speed for flying over the reed bed where it lives. Being so slow, it misses nothing. It spots its prey and then it drops softly on the creature below. And then its day's hunting is done.

The marsh harriers went extinct in Britain, as breeding birds, for a number of reasons. First, many of their wet places were drained for farmland. Secondly, many were shot. It was a normal thing, to shoot all birds of prey, in case they killed the animals humans like to kill for fun, birds like pheasants and partridges.

But the real problem was chemicals. Farmers used a chemical called DDT to kill the insects that ate their crops. This damaged the insects, and damaged the animals that ate the insects. But most of all, it damaged the animals that ate the animals that ate the insects.

Birds of prey suffered most.

The trouble was that DDT built up in the bodies of the insect-eaters. That meant that it built up even more in the bodies of the birds of prey. And it had a strange effect. It made them unable to lay proper strong eggs. The eggs they laid were horribly fragile. They just broke. So the birds could not breed successfully in Britain. Extinction had to follow.

But now there is a decent population of marsh harriers: and all kinds of birds of prey have increased in numbers in Britain. The marsh harriers have moved into new wet and reedy places that have been created by conservation organisations. People are now more responsible about shooting birds of prey: it still goes on, but the animals are now protected by law. And the law is fairly well enforced.

But the best news is that DDT and some of the more dangerous

MARSH HARRIER
Scientific name: *Circus aeruginosus*
Size: length up to 56 cm (22 in.) plus tail 20 cm (8 in.)
wing span up to 130 cm (51 in.)
Range: Europe, Middle East
Habitat: around shallow standing waters
Food: marsh mammals, birds

insecticides have been banned. This is good news for birds of prey in Britain, and likewise for birds of prey in much of Europe and North America. However, DDT is still manufactured and used in many countries of the world. It's dangerous: it's also cheap.

But the fact remains that the marsh harrier shows the way ahead. The birds have spread back to Britain from elsewhere in Europe. And where they found a place they could breed, they did so. Enough of them managed to breed without being shot: and the eggs were strong and successful, now that the problem of DDT has been removed.

The marsh harrier was an animal that conservationists had despaired about. They thought that a healthy population of all kinds of birds of prey was a thing of the past. Now, in Britain, the bird of prey population is better than it has been for years. Once again, hurrah.

92 Southern right whale

THERE are two species of whales that are called right whales. This name always used to puzzle me. Perhaps it meant something to do with right-handedness. The northern right whale and the **southern right whale** – what was so right about them?

I should have known. They were called right whales because they were the right whales to kill. They swim very slowly, so they are easy to harpoon. And they are absolutely packed with the things that whales are killed for: oil and whalebone.

The right whale to kill: the northern right whale was the first whale to be hunted, and it has been hunted for about 1,000 years. The whales used to gather in huge groups: but hunting has almost done away with them. They are just about hanging on.

After the whale-hunters had hunted the northern right whale close to extinction, they moved south, and there they found the southern right whale. Full-scale hunting of the southern right whale began

round about the start of the nineteenth century: in about 70 years, these too had almost gone.

There was no longer any point in hunting them. And as long ago as 1935, hunting the southern right whale was made illegal in international law. However, hunting still continued in secret; mostly, it was ships from the former Soviet empire that did the damage.

But now even this has stopped. And the numbers of southern right whales are going up at a quite astonishing rate. It is reckoned that they are increasing by as much as nine per cent every year. Now it must be said that the numbers are still only about one-tenth of what the total population once was, before the whalers moved in a couple of hundred years ago. But it is still remarkable, and still worth a huge cheer.

The northern right whale has shown no such recovery. Partly, this is because it lives around the coast, and so the animals are often injured by ships. And perhaps the numbers are too low to recover at all: they live on, but perhaps they're already doomed to extinction. Species like this have been termed 'the living dead'.

But the southern right whale is emphatically not a member of the living dead. It is alive and lively and going from strength to strength. Off the coast of South Africa, whale watchers can see this animal in heart-lifting numbers.

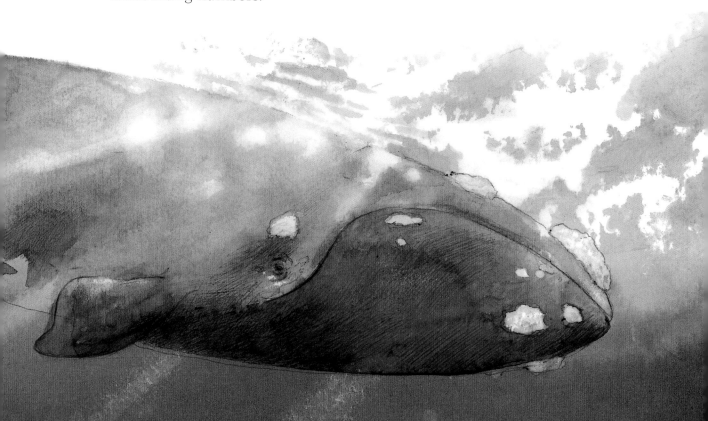

The problems of whales are not over, despite protection. Two countries, Norway and Japan, still insist on killing whales. There is nothing like the killing of the old days, in which as many as 1,000,000 whales of all species were killed every year. But whales have been reduced to such small numbers that any hunting at all is a threat to the future of the species.

The best news is that the subject of whaling is a strong and emotional one, and many countries in the world are prepared to stand up for whales. A whale sanctuary has been declared in all the waters around the Antarctic, and there is talk of making an entire global ocean sanctuary for the whales.

Save the whales! This was one of the rallying cries of the conservation movement as it began to gather pace in the 1960s. It even became a kind of joke. There is much that can go wrong, but in terms of the southern right whale at least – well, we *have* saved the whales. They would already be extinct, or at best among the living dead, had the conservation movement not stepped in. The next task is to make sure they stay with us. The southern right whale is increasing. Hurrah.

SOUTHERN RIGHT WHALE
Scientific name: *Eubalaena australis*
Size: length up to 10 m (33 ft)
Range: southern oceans
Habitat: ocean
Food: small crustaceans

93 Eurasian otter

WE know that the task of putting Humpty Dumpty together again is impossible. But that's no reason not to try. It's not the answer to conservation, for that way madness lies. We cannot accept the idea that 'it doesn't matter if we destroy a place because we can always build it back again.'

But once something *has* been destroyed, that doesn't mean we should give up. We must simply do our best to restore nature. We do so knowing that we can never do the job properly. All we can do is our best.

And sometimes, our best goes a very long way. That is certainly the case with the **Eurasian otter.** The otter was once common in the rivers of Britain: but it reached the edge of extinction. Now it's coming back. And it's coming back because humans, and human organisations, have been doing their best to fight the Humpty Dumpty Effect.

EURASIAN OTTER
Scientific name: *Lutra lutra*
Size: length up to 120 cm (47 in.)
weight up to 9 kg (19 lb)
Range: most of Europe and Asia
Habitat: rivers
Food: fish

Otters live in rivers, and eat fish. It stands to reason that if you poison the rivers with filth and kill all the fish, you are not going to get any otters. And that is the history of the otter in Britain. In all countries, everywhere in the world, rivers have been treated as waste disposal units. People throw their rubbish into the river, and it gets washed away.

But there came a point, as factories and farms grew larger, when the rivers simply couldn't take any more. Rivers everywhere became stinking open sewers, full of human waste and rubbish of all kinds. Factories poured their stink into the nearest bit of moving water: so did farms. Rivers in Wales ran black, stained with the dust from the coal mines. The rivers could no longer provide a home for living things. The rivers were almost dead.

Meanwhile, humans, with their mania for tidiness, set about organising the rivers. They were made to flow where it was convenient for humans, and at the sort of depths that humans wanted. Wild rivers became almost unknown. Rivers became tame canals that flowed between banks that humans had built for them. And the fish suffered, and as is always the way with top predators, the fish-eaters suffered still more. Black rivers: and a black situation for the otters.

Now there are more otters than there have been for years. Otters

are returning to their old places. This is largely because the rivers are clean again, and filled with fish. Humans have actually seen the danger of poisoning rivers. If we poison our rivers, we are poisoning our planet and ourselves. Now there are laws to prevent the dumping of poisons and filth, and the laws are enforced. Clean rivers are once again teeming with good healthy fish.

The last stage of the big clean-up was to bring back the top predator: by making the rivers otter-friendly. Rivers have been allowed to run wilder in some places: with deep pools and bubbling, rushing shallows. Otter hideaways have been built by humans.

There are problems still. A chemical used to keep sheep free of parasites is bringing a new poison into the rivers. Many otters are killed by cars when they travel away from their rivers. But the fact is that there are now plenty of otters about. The main reason for this is water: good clean water.

I once saw three otters playing at the water's edge, and diving back in to continue their game. They are among the world's most delightful animals. And they give us a very special message: that the water is good and clean and full of life again. The otters could not be there if that was not true. Hurrah for otters: hurrah for clean rivers.

94 Whooping crane

WHENEVER there is pressure between people and the wild world, it seems that the soft and soggy places disappear first. Fresh water is too valuable for humans; and the land that is left after a piece of wetland has been drained is often very good for farming. What's more, a piece of really good wetland seems to offend something very deep in human beings. It is wild, it is uncivilised. A large area of wetland looks almost like a human failure: an area of complete waste. An opportunity for development: wasted.

The more developed the country, the fewer of these opportunities to drain wetlands have been wasted. We have already looked at the draining of the fens in Britain, which means that there is nowhere for the bittern to live. In North America, the same pattern has continued.

There was once a vast area of wetland, a patchwork of marshes that stretched from southern Canada into the US, and these marshes were the home of the **whooping crane**. If ever there was a bird to

WHOOPING CRANE
Scientific name: *Grus americanus*
Size: head and body length up to 151 cm (59.5 in.)
weight up to 7.3 kg (16 lb)
Range: US
Habitat: wetland
Food: snails, insect larvae, frogs, leeches, fish, rodents

stand for the loss of wetland, it is this one. A whooping crane needs two separate areas of wetland: those in the north, where it comes to breed in the summer, and another set of marshes, down south in the Gulf of Mexico, where it spends the colder months of the year.

The huge areas of marsh both north and south naturally held huge numbers of cranes. But then the marshes were drained and turned into farmland, and the cranes lost their breeding grounds and their wintering grounds. There wasn't just a decline in numbers: the species plummeted to the edge of disaster. By 1941, there were either 15 or 16 left; the records are confused on the exact number. Either way, extinction was just around the corner.

It was time once again for conservationists to do battle with Humpty Dumpty. A breeding programme was started in 1975 and protection of the crucial breeding and wintering sites was established. The population has grown again. There are now more than 140 wild birds, plus three flocks in captivity. It is slow going, but at least it's going.

This is a success story, and that's always something to cheer about. But conservation never stops. It is a job that never ends: as soon as we take our eyes off an endangered species, we're likely to find it gone. The cranes are great travellers, and they fly vast distances between their summer and their winter grounds. Their stopover places on this long journey are as important as the main grounds themselves:

for the birds need to rest, and to feed, to fuel themselves for the next stage on their colossal journey. If they can't do this, they will never make it. And no conservation organisation can control every flap of a journey of a few thousand miles.

Hunting used to be a serious problem for these birds, as they made their big journeys, but now that is more or less under control. The main danger is overhead electricity cables: the birds fly into them, and are killed. There is also a problem with the birds' wintering ground in Texas. Oil exploration continues here. If there is a major find, and people move in to drill for oil, the disturbance this will cause and the loss of the wetland is likely to spell the end of the species.

The whooping crane is a bird that has been brought back from the very edge. America is full of stories of its wild past, its wild places, its wild west. But the fact of the matter is that there are fewer and fewer wild places left in the country: and many of these are in danger. America needs its wild places. And so does every other nation on Earth. But the efforts to save the whooping crane have made some of the wet and wild places safe, at least for the time being. It is another small hurrah.

95 Mauritius kestrel

CONSERVATION works. Sometimes the problems are massive: sometimes it looks as if the only thing to do is to give up. But giving up is not the only thing; only the easiest thing. The hard way is hope: and making hope work. The **Mauritius kestrel** is a striking example of hope rewarded. Hope, with a great deal of hard work. And money, of course.

The Mauritius kestrel is one of those island species: as we have seen in this book, a group of birds reaches an island and over the years, separated from the rest of the population, it becomes a new species. Kestrels are small, dashing falcons. In most of the world, kestrel species specialise in hovering, that is to say, flying in the same spot, not moving forward or back, and then dropping onto their prey. The Mauritius kestrel has shorter, more rounded wings than its relatives, and it specialises in dashing through the treetops, taking small creatures by surprise. It eats large insects, small birds, and reptiles.

Now Mauritius is a good island when it comes to talking about conservation. Mauritius was the home of the dodo. The name dodo means idiot: the bird was such a fool that it trusted humans. Humans killed the trusting birds for food, and they didn't even run away. Humans owe the island of Mauritius a bird or two.

By 1973, the world population of the Mauritius kestrel was down to six, two of them in captivity. The reasons for the decline are complicated. One reason was pesticides, especially DDT, the same problem that faced the marsh harrier. Then there was the problem of forest destruction, and the introduction of foreign trees, less suitable

MAURITIUS KESTREL
Scientific name: *Falco punctatus*
Size: total length up to 26 cm (10 in.)
weight up to 110 g (3.0 oz)
Range: Mauritius
Habitat: forest
Food: small reptiles, birds, large insects

for the animals of Mauritius. This meant that there were fewer small animals for the Mauritius kestrel to eat. As we know, the top predator always suffers first.

Then the conservationists stepped in. They began the rescue programme for the Mauritius kestrel in 1973, and it was based on captive breeding. Some of these birds were bred from captive parents; others were reared from eggs taken from the nests of wild birds. Then the birds were released into the wild and, to everybody's delight, they thrived.

By 1994, there were 68 wild pairs of Mauritius kestrels, and a wild population of 250 individual birds. The birds were thriving once again: and it is anticipated that the population will continue to grow, until there are about 600 wild birds. This is nothing like the previous level of population, of course. The dense evergreen forests that once covered the island have mostly been felled. There are only small patches of forest left: islands within an island. But the fact of the matter is that the Mauritius kestrel faced what looked like certain extinction. And thanks to quite colossal efforts, it has come back from the edge.

Island populations are vulnerable, as we know. But the very smallness of islands makes the problem itself a small one: a problem to which you can see a solution. The entire planet is like Mauritius: vulnerable and full of troubles. We must apply the Mauritius solution. That is to say, great effort, much money, great hope, and the overwhelming desire to succeed. That way, there will be more hurrahs to come.

96 Juan Fernandez fur seal

WE have just given a hurrah for the Mauritius kestrel, which was and is a triumph for the people who work in conservation. Now let's turn to our next animal worth cheering – the **Juan Fernandez fur seal**. And the survival of this species is a triumph for – well, nobody. But there are something like 12,000 Juan Fernanadez fur seals in the world, and the numbers continue to grow – and that's not bad going for an animal that was thought to be extinct.

No: real human effort has not gone into saving the Juan Fernandez fur seal. The big effort went into trying to kill them off. This was an animal whose world population was once several million. It takes a lot of time and trouble to reduce several million to virtually nothing, but humans have always been able to take time and trouble.

The seal lives on only a few islands off the coast of Chile in South America, the Juan Fernandez islands and the Deventuradas group. They were first discovered at the end of the seventeenth century and, after about a hundred years or so, most of them had gone. They were killed for their meat and for their fur. Killing seals is one of the easiest jobs in the world: a seal on land cannot run very far or very fast. And seals must come ashore to breed. It's hardly hunting. In fact, it has been called harvesting, as if the seals were fruit, or ears of corn. Certainly, a seal on land is ripe for the plucking. And the Juan Fernandez fur seal is a particularly easy animal to kill, even by seal standards,

because it spends most of its year in and around its breeding grounds.

And so the Juan Fernandez fur seal was reckoned to be extinct by 1950: another victim of the bottomless bucket principle, another example of the tragedy of the commons. But later the odd seal was spotted, and then a small colony of 200 was discovered.

And what was done? Pretty well nothing. And it was enough. The seal population began to climb again. The wearing of sealskin became unfashionable. This was partly because the press printed horrific pictures of baby seals of all species being clubbed to death. The wearing of all kinds of wild animal skins was no longer fashionable in many places in the rich parts of the world. There was a general feeling that the time of slaughter should end; that the time of conservation should begin.

In simple terms, many people in the world felt that killing baby seals was bad: and that not killing baby seals was good. And this vague feeling was enough to allow the Juan Fernandez fur seal to

JUAN FERNANDEZ FUR SEAL
Scientific name: *Arctocephalus philippii*
Size: (males) length up to 2 m (6.5 ft)
weight up to 140 kg (309 lb)
Range: Chile
Habitat: seas and islands
Food: fish, squid, octopus

build up its numbers again.

There are still problems. There always are. The seal is now protected by Chilean law, but a number are killed by fishermen, who resent the fact that seals also hunt for fish. A long-term problem is the health of the fishing grounds. Overfishing of the waters will mean no food for seals, as well as no livelihood for fishermen. The solution, for both the seals and the fishermen, is to avoid the tragedy of the commons, and to control fishing, so that there will be fish in the seas in the future years, for both humans and seals.

This is not a story of conservation. It is a story of letting well alone. In some cases, letting well alone is all that a species needs. Simply not being killed in vast numbers is enough to allow a recovery. Given an even break, any species is a good bet for survival. When at all possible, life continues. Which is what this book is about: so hurrah for the Juan Fernandez fur seal.

97 Arabian oryx

WE began this book with a sad story about a unicorn, and now, as we move into the closing stages, it is time for a happy story about a unicorn. We began with the plight of the scimitar-horned oryx. Let's move towards the finish with the **Arabian oryx**. This animal has already been extinct once.

Extinct in the wild, of course. Like its scimitar-horned relation, the Arabian oryx is a desert animal: a miracle of survival. It has been known to survive for 22 months without a drink; it has even been known to travel 155 kilometres to reach an area of desert where it had rained.

And it was wiped out for fun. Hunters killed them. Not skilled hunters, people who tracked them across miles of desert and brought them down with a single shot. Not hungry hunters, who wanted meat to feed their families. No: hunters of the Arabian oryx chased them in powerful 4-wheel drive vehicles, and then mowed them down with automatic weapons. That wasn't sport, but a massacre.

In the end, it was just one more extinction in the long episode of extinctions caused by humans. But there were still a handful of Arabian oryx left in captivity, and a handful of conservationists who hoped to turn back the clock.

The remains of the last wild Arabian oryx were found in the desert in 1972. But by this time, the conservationists had already moved in. They had captured three of the last wild animals left. These were joined by four more from various zoos: the world herd of oryx. All seven of them. They were brought together at Phoenix Zoo in the US,

because the climate is similar to that of the Arabian oryx's homeland, the deserts of the Arabian peninsula.

The conservationists acquired the best possible ally. This was the Sultan of Oman. He decided that he wanted the Arabian oryx to return to its rightful home. He was determined to protect a wild herd, if one could be re-established. In 1980, members of the captive-bred herd were taken to Oman. There they spent two more years in captivity – and then at last they were released.

A few more oryx were released in the following years. Today there are more than 300 Arabian oryx in the wild, and all but 22 of them were actually born in the wild. The oryx are looked after by rangers: the desert is now very well patrolled and well guarded. And though some are occasionally killed by hunters, the fact is that the oryx are looked after and the laws that protect them are taken seriously. If an animal becomes a Sultan's pride and joy, then it has a better chance of surviving than most.

The story of the Arabian oryx is a tale of triumph. And in one way, it is a tale of triumph I hope never to hear again. The way forward is not to think that if animals go extinct, they can be brought back. The answer is not to send them extinct in the first place. The answer is to make them the people's pride and joy long before there are none of them left. Captive breeding and re-release can work with some species, and that is wonderful. But it is not the way forward. The story of the oryx is one of the great hurrahs of conservation history: and we cannot help but join in with the cheering. The Arabian oryx has been returned to the wild. The next step is to try and return the world to its senses.

ARABIAN ORYX
Scientific name: *Oryx leucoryx*
Size: weight up to 90 kg (198 lb)
Range: Oman
Habitat: desert
Food: desert vegetation

98 White rhinoceros

IN the end, you can bring extinction down to two very simple ideas. Humans cause extinctions: first, by killing animals and second, by destroying the places where animals live.

Let's take the first idea first: humans cause extinctions by killing animals. And since we're now on number nine of our top ten good-news stories, let's look at the way in which the problem of humans killing animals can be solved. Let's look at the **white rhinoceros**.

The white rhinoceros is one of the two African species of rhino, and it is not white at all. The name comes from a confusion with the South African word *wijde*, which means wide. The white rhino has a wide mouth, good for eating grass; the black rhino has a pointy mouth with a hooked upper lip, very good for stripping the leaves off branches and twigs.

There are two sub-species of white rhino, the northern and the southern white rhinoceros. The two could breed together, and produce young capable of breeding in their turn – but under normal circumstances they would never meet in the wild. The populations live too far apart. They have grown separate, and because of various slight differences, they are called sub-species.

It's the southern sub-species we will concentrate on. At the end of the nineteenth century, the southern white rhino was thought to be extinct; mostly because of reckless over-hunting. Now there is a population of more than 7,000. And that, I think, counts as a success story.

WHITE RHINOCEROS
Scientific name: *Ceratotherium simum*
Size: head and body length up to 4.2 m (13.8 ft)
Range: South Africa, Zimbabwe, Zaire
Habitat: open country
Food: grass

Rhinos all over the word are killed for their horns, as we saw when we looked at the black rhinoceros. There are miles and miles of good habitat for black rhinos, with no black rhinos. If they were put in there, they would very soon be killed.

South Africa is one of the least wild countries in Africa, but it still has its national parks, and these have been very well guarded. Those who would kill rhinos for their horns – which are wanted as ceremonial dagger handles, and to make traditional Chinese medicines – simply cannot get into the parks to do it.

Killing rhinos is against the law, but as we have seen again and again, it's one thing making a law, and quite another making people keep the law. In South Africa the law has been enforced. It's sad that the only way to save the animal has been to put a fence round wild places, and to fill them with men who enforce the law, and keep people out. But that has brought good news for the white rhino.

The next step is to change the world's attitude to the rhinoceros: to reach an agreement across the world that a rhinoceros horn does more for the world when it is worn on the nose of a rhino than it does when it is ground up in a box, or carved up into a fancy shape. And I know this sounds like a hard thing to do, but consider. Just a few years ago, film stars wore leopardskin coats and no one said anything against them. No film star would dare wear a leopardskin coat now: the world would hate her for it.

People do change; the world can change its mind. The important thing is to make people change their minds while there are still animals there to save. And the white rhino is, against the odds, there to provide our ninth hurrah.

99 Siberian tiger

ET'S say it one last time: humans cause extinctions by killing animals; they also cause extinctions by destroying the places where animals live. Pity the poor animal when it suffers both. And that is the case with many species: it's certainly true of the tiger, an animal we met as number three in this bestiary.

We have talked about tigers before: but I'm going to break my own rules. We have looked at tigers, and enjoyed their beauty, and been saddened by the fact that the tiger's is a bad-news story. Well, now we are going to meet tigers again. And we're going to cheer for a good-news story.

I have broken one rule, about meeting the same animal twice. Now I will break another, and consider not a species of animal, but a sub-species. This is one of the eight sub-species of tiger, and it happens to be a very good-news story indeed. So let's say a hurrah for the **Siberian tiger**.

There are eight sub-species of tiger: three of these are already extinct. The Siberian tiger hangs on. It was thought to be hanging on by a thread: because it was hunted, because its wild places were not looked after, because tiger-bones fetch a high price. They are wanted, as we know, for making tiger-bone wine, for Chinese medicines.

It was thought that there were no more than a couple of hundred of them left, but a new investigation shows that there are more than twice that many: about 500. And there is more good news: practically all these tigers live in the same place – 95 per cent of them, in fact. This makes Siberian tigers the largest single group of tigers left in the world today.

We think of Siberia as a land of perpetual snow, but this is not the case. There is a huge wild area of forest called the taiga (pronounced just the same as the beast we are discussing). And though the area is threatened by logging and mining, there are still endless miles; endless miles of wilderness. There the Siberian tiger lives, and makes its living by eating wild pigs.

Although it's true that some Siberian tigers are killed by poachers, who sell the corpses to the Chinese medicine trade, the huge size and the wildness of the area makes it impossible for the tigers to be wiped out by the current numbers of poachers. Partly, this is because there are so many tigers there. Most of the tigers in the world live in small patches of land. The Siberian tiger is probably the only sub-species of tiger that does not face the central problem of the island species: the fact that one disaster could wipe out a population. Poaching is a disaster all right: but at current numbers, the Siberian tiger seems able to cope.

And the good news here is obvious: if you don't destroy the wild places, the chances are that the animals living in them won't be destroyed either. In many areas of conservation, in many areas of life, the best possible solution to the problem is letting well alone. If humans can only leave the taiga alone, then with luck (and better control of the poachers) the tiger will be safe. If we can save the wilderness areas we have left, then we are more than half way towards solving the problems of wildlife and conservation.

Humans used to fear wilderness. Now we are learning to love it. The more we destroy our wilderness, the more precious is the stuff that is left: and the more we are able to appreciate it. I think we have now destroyed enough to be able to appreciate every last little morsel of wilderness we have. If we can stop destroying things now, it's not too late – and certainly not too late for the Siberian tiger.

The Siberian tiger is the biggest cat on Earth today. If we let the tiger go extinct, we know we really have failed. It's perhaps the number one animal on the must-save list. The – relatively – huge population of the Siberian tiger is enough to finish this top ten, and to give us our last hurrah.

SIBERIAN TIGER
Scientific name: *Panthera tigris altaica*
Size: length up to 2.8 m (9.2 ft)
weight up to 306 kg (675 lb)
Range: Siberia
Habitat: open wooded country known as taiga
Food: mammals, mainly wild pigs

100 Human

FOR animal number 100, the last in the bestiary, let us turn to a large mammal. It is one hundred times more numerous than any land mammal of similar size has ever been in the entire history of life. It is ecologically abnormal. It is a huge success story: and yet the species stands in the most colossal danger. It could become the first species to destroy itself; the first species to make itself extinct. It is the human; what else?

Humans are destroying the planet, which is bad news for all the animals that live on the planet. And humans are just one more animal on planet Earth. An exceptional animal: a unique animal, no doubt about that. But that will not be enough to save the humans. If humans destroy the planet, then humans destroy themselves.

Throughout history, humans have prided themselves on how different they are from other animals, how far they are from nature. It's time to put the entire history of ideas into reverse. If humans cannot come to terms with the fact that they are animals, that they are part of nature, then humans will destroy themselves.

Humans depend on other species for their existence. Life is not possible for humans without many other living things. For example, we need trees to produce oxygen and to disperse carbon monoxide: we can't even breathe without the help of other species. The great forests of the world make it possible for humans to breathe: and humans are destroying forests as fast as they can.

Humans need other species to decompose sewage. Humans would poison themselves without these creatures. Humans need other species to produce food, to make the soil fertile, to provide wood, even to provide the paper for this book.

Should humans simply look after the various useful species, then?

This argument is not even worth bothering with. No one single ecosystem on Earth is predictable. Ecosystems are far too complicated. How many extinctions are necessary before an ecosystem collapses? How many ecosystems need to collapse before all ecosystems are affected? We don't know. We dare not risk it. We have just the one planet. There is only one experiment. If it fails, we cannot start again.

The fact is that all life on Earth is connected, and that when we harm one bit of the Earth, or one species, then we cause harm to all. Including ourselves.

Humans have always thought they were better than other species. Well, the main difference between humans, the Siberian tiger and the no-eyed big-eyed wolf spider is that humans have the power to destroy their own places, and the power to destroy the places of every other species on the planet. We will only succeed in being better than these species – better, as opposed to more powerful – if we stop the destruction.

And that is the answer, for the planet, for the species with which humans share the planet, and for humans themselves. Just stop. Because it is humans – nothing and no one else – that have caused the wave of extinctions that has been sweeping across the planet for

HUMAN
Scientific name: *Homo sapiens*
Size: (adult) about 1.9m (6 ft)
Range: everywhere
Habitat: anywhere
Food: various

the past 40,000 years or so.

And that's good news, not bad news. Why? Because we can just stop doing it. We can't change the weather, or the path of the Earth relative to the sun, or the flight of asteroids across space. But we can stop killing things. We can stop destroying wilderness. We can just stop.

Other species enrich our lives, warm our hearts. They also make our lives possible; fill our lungs. We could bring everything down to one single wildlife campaign: save the humans! Because the best way to do this is to save every other species that lives on Earth today.

What shall we do? First, believe in the importance of life on Earth, all life on this planet. And enjoy it. You probably already do both: well, good.

And then join organisations: there are some names and addresses on page 272. Humans can do more when they work together: that is what organisations are all about. And also, share your pleasure in wildlife with those that are interested. Quietly spread the word.

And one more thing – don't give up. Don't get depressed. Keep on hoping.

Giving up is the worst crime in conservation, in life. And there is plenty of good news in conservation, plenty of hope. There is an old saying: where there is life, there is hope. It works the other way round, too. Where there is hope, there is life.

Useful contacts

This book leaves its reader with a question: what can I do about it? The answer is simple: enjoy wildlife. The more you know, the more you enjoy. Some readers may end up working in conservation: I hope so. And I hope that all readers will become and remain supporters of conservation. The best way of supporting conservation is, again, by enjoying wildlife. And part of that is to join conservation organisations.

Worldwide Fund for Nature
Panda House
Weyside Park
Godalming
Surrey
GU7 1XR

Royal Society for the Protection of Birds
The Lodge
Sandy
Bedfordshire
SG19 2DL

Birdlife International
32 Cambridge Road
Girton
Cambridgeshire
CB3 0PJ

British readers may want to join their country wildlife trust.
These can be located via:
The Wildlife Trusts
The Green
Witham Park
Waterside South
Lincoln
LN5 7JR